AN ATHLETE'S GUIDE TO BUILD CONFIDENCE

NOELL GRANT

FIRST EDITION: 2025

ISBN: HARDCOVER 979-8-9927039-0-0
       PAPERBACK 979-8-9927039-1-7
       EBOOK 979-8-9927039-3-1

LIBRARY OF CONGRESS CONTROL NUMBER: 2025908313

COVER DESIGN BY NOELL GRANT

FOR PERMISSIONS OR INQUIRIES, CONTACT: NOELL GRANT AT NOELLGRANTBOOKS@GMAIL.COM.

"CHANGE YOUR
MINDSET
BUILD YOUR
CONFIDENCE,
ELEVATE
YOUR GAME."

-NOELL GRANT, AUTHOR

DEDICATION

I dedicate this book to all the hard-working and dedicated athletes. I trust you will discover your sacrifices today will lead to your future freedom.

-Noell Grant,
Author

FOREWORD

IN 1995, I MET NOELL GRANT WHEN SHE JOINED MY COLLEGE BASKETBALL TEAM. FROM THE MOMENT SHE STEPPED ONTO THE COURT, IT WAS CLEAR THAT SHE EMBODIED THREE DEFINING QUALITIES: FAST, STRONG, AND TENACIOUS. THESE TRAITS SET HER APART THEN, AND THEY CONTINUE TO DEFINE HER TODAY. WE WERE MEMBERS OF A CLOSE-KNIT TEAM THAT LIVED, BREATHED, AND DREAMED BASKETBALL, ALL UNDER THE LEADERSHIP OF COACH ED DAVIS WHO WAS A MASTER AT ONE THING-FIGURING OUT HOW TO WIN THE GAME. OUR TEAM ACHIEVED NATIONAL NCAA RECOGNITION, CONSISTENTLY RANKED AT THE TOP IN SEVERAL CATEGORIES. ONE OF OUR PROUDEST MOMENTS WAS WINNING THE FIRST CIAA CHAMPIONSHIP FOR BOWIE STATE UNIVERSITY—A MILESTONE THAT REMAINS A HIGHLIGHT IN BOTH OF OUR LIVES.

OVER THE YEARS, NOELL AND I HAVE REMAINED CLOSE, NOT JUST AS FRIENDS BUT ALSO AS BUSINESS PARTNERS. SHE SERVED AS THE CHIEF OPERATING OFFICER OF MIPOH (MY PURSUIT OF HAPPINESS), A CORPORATE WELLNESS COMPANY THAT PARTNERS WITH ORGANIZATIONS TO PROVIDE WELLNESS SERVICES THAT IMPROVE HEALTH AND HAPPINESS FOR THEIR EMPLOYEES. OUR PARTNERSHIP, BORN ON THE BASKETBALL COURT, IS BUILT ON MUTUAL RESPECT, SHARED VALUES, AND AN UNWAVERING COMMITMENT TO EXCELLENCE.

IT IS WITH GREAT HONOR THAT I INTRODUCE THIS BOOK. THE WISDOM AND PRACTICAL ADVICE THAT NOELL OFFERS THROUGHOUT ITS PAGES ARE INVALUABLE TO ANYONE STRIVING FOR GREATNESS—WHETHER IN SPORTS OR IN LIFE. THROUGH VIVID ILLUSTRATIONS AND ENCOURAGING MESSAGES, SHE SPEAKS FROM THE HEART OF A CHAMPION, OFFERING INSIGHTS THAT WILL INSPIRE, CHALLENGE, AND MOTIVATE YOU TO TAKE A DEEPER LOOK WITHIN YOURSELF AND DISCOVER YOUR "ALL-STAR HEART."

TALKING ABOUT A WINNING ATTITUDE IS ONE THING, BUT WALKING THE WALK IS WHERE TRUE WISDOM IS BORN. NOELL GRANT PULLS NO PUNCHES IN THIS BOOK. HER WORDS ARE THE GUT SHOT YOU MAY NEED TO WAKE UP AND SEIZE YOUR OPPORTUNITY. SHE KNOWS WHAT IT TAKES TO GRIND, SWEAT, AND GET DOWN ON THE FLOOR TO REACH THE TOP. WINNING BEGINS IN THE MIND. IT STARTS WITH FAITH, GROWS INTO BELIEF, AND ULTIMATELY BLOSSOMS INTO UNSHAKABLE CONFIDENCE IN ONESELF.

AS YOU TURN EACH PAGE, I ENCOURAGE YOU TO REFLECT ON THE MESSAGES THAT RESONATE WITH YOU. WHEN DOUBT CREEPS IN, READ IT AGAIN AND FIND THE GEM THAT SPEAKS TO YOUR JOURNEY. THE WISDOM YOU SEEK IS WAITING FOR YOU IN THESE PAGES. SHARE YOUR THOUGHTS AND LEARNINGS.

START CONVERSATIONS WITH YOUR TEAM ABOUT WHERE YOU ARE AND WHERE YOU WANT TO BE. DECIDE WHO YOU ARE—DON'T LET SOMEONE ELSE DEFINE YOU. WRITE YOUR OWN HISTORY BY LIVING YOUR FULLEST LIFE. MASTERING YOUR MIND IS THE KEY TO LIVING A LIFE BEYOND YOUR WILDEST DREAMS. WHOEVER YOU ARE WHEN YOU WALK ONTO THE COURT WILL NEVER BE THE SAME WHEN YOU WALK OFF—EACH PRACTICE, WORKOUT AND GAME WILL CHANGE YOU. BUT IT TAKES EFFORT AND A DEEP DESIRE FOR CHANGE TO BE YOUR BEST. CHANGE IS UNPREDICTABLE, UNFAMILIAR, AND OFTEN UNCOMFORTABLE, BUT YOU HAVE TO WANT IT AND GO AFTER IT WITH EVERYTHING YOU HAVE AND EVERYTHING YOU ARE. ONLY THEN WILL YOU MAXIMIZE YOUR POTENTIAL. THAT'S WHAT REAL WINNING LOOKS LIKE.

AS A YOUNG ATHLETE PASSIONATE ABOUT BASKETBALL, THE SPORT WAS MY OUTLET FOR MENTAL FREEDOM, AUTHENTIC EXPRESSION AND THE UNBRIDLED URGE TO SEE THE RESULTS OF MY EFFORTS. I LOVED BASKETBALL WITH A PASSION AND I THOUGHT MY RELATIONSHIP WITH IT WOULD LAST FOREVER. FOR A TIME, BASKETBALL WAS MY WAY OF EXPRESSING MYSELF TO THE WORLD. I WAS CONFIDENT, UNAPOLOGETIC, AND RESOLUTE IN MY SHOOTING. BUT THERE WAS A WEAKNESS IN MY GAME THAT I CHOSE NOT TO ADDRESS BECAUSE IT WAS UNCOMFORTABLE AND DIFFICULT.

FOREWORD

THIS CHOICE ULTIMATELY ENDED MY DREAM OF HAPPILY EVER AFTER ON THE BASKETBALL COURT BUT GAVE BIRTH TO A NEW ELEVATED MINDSET AND PERSPECTIVE ABOUT MY LIFE. THIS LESSON CONTINUES TO SERVE AS A REMINDER TO LIVE IN THE MOMENT, TO BE PRESENT AND TO MAXIMIZE MY POTENTIAL IN EVERYTHING I DO. THIS LESSON ALSO GAVE ME THE STRENGTH AND RESOLVE TO RESIGN FROM AN AMAZING JOB AND DEDICATE MY LIFE TO HELPING OTHERS IN THEIR PURSUIT OF HAPPINESS. I HAVE LEARNED TO BE GRATEFUL FOR TOUGH LESSONS AND THE HARD KNOCKS!

NOELL'S JOURNEY, SHARED IN THIS BOOK, IS A TESTAMENT TO THE POWER OF ADDRESSING WEAKNESSES, EMBRACING DISCOMFORT, AND PUSHING BEYOND LIMITS TO ACHIEVE GREATNESS. HER STORY WILL RESONATE WITH ANYONE WHO HAS EVER FACED ADVERSITY, DOUBTED THEMSELVES, OR STRUGGLED TO REACH THEIR FULL POTENTIAL. THIS BOOK IS MORE THAN JUST A GUIDE TO WINNING IN SPORTS—IT'S A BLUEPRINT FOR WINNING IN LIFE.

THE REASON I'M WRITING THIS FOREWORD FOR NOELL IS SIMPLE: I'VE SEEN HER EMBODY THE PRINCIPLES SHE WRITES ABOUT, BOTH ON AND OFF THE COURT. I'VE WITNESSED HER GRIT, DETERMINATION, AND UNWAVERING COMMITMENT TO EXCELLENCE.

SHE LIVES THE LESSONS SHE SHARES, AND THAT'S WHAT MAKES THIS BOOK SO POWERFUL. NOELL DOESN'T JUST TALK ABOUT WINNING—SHE SHOWS YOU HOW TO LIVE IT.

AS YOU DELVE INTO THESE PAGES, YOU'LL FIND THE TOOLS, INSPIRATION, AND WISDOM YOU NEED TO OVERCOME OBSTACLES, PUSH YOUR LIMITS, AND ACHIEVE GREATNESS. WHETHER YOU'RE AN ATHLETE, A PROFESSIONAL, OR SOMEONE SEEKING PERSONAL GROWTH, THIS BOOK HAS SOMETHING VALUABLE TO OFFER. TAKE IT TO HEART, APPLY ITS LESSONS, AND YOU'LL FIND YOURSELF EQUIPPED TO WIN IN EVERY ASPECT OF YOUR LIFE.

I WISH YOU PEACE AND POWER ON YOUR JOURNEY IN PURSUIT OF THE HAPPINESS YOU SEEK AND THE SUCCESS YOU DREAM OF IN YOUR SPORT AND IN LIFE. BE WELL MY FRIEND.

DAWN HANCOCK,
FOUNDER & CEO

mipoh

DAWN HANCOCK & NOELL GRANT
BOWIE STATE UNIVERSITY, 1996-1997

BACKED BY A DEGREE IN SOCIOLOGY, A CHAMPIONSHIP-WINNING BASKETBALL CAREER, AND OVER TWO DECADES OF EXPERIENCE AS A POLICE OFFICER, I'VE SPENT MY LIFE STUDYING HUMAN BEHAVIOR—UNDER PRESSURE, IN COMPETITION, AND IN CRISIS. MY MISSION IS TO HELP ATHLETES BREAK MENTAL BARRIERS, SHIFT THEIR MINDSET, AND UNLOCK THEIR FULL POTENTIAL; NOT JUST IN THE GAME, BUT IN LIFE. I BELIEVE CONFIDENCE IS THE KEY TO SUCCESS IN SPORTS. BY BOOSTING YOUR CONFIDENCE, YOU WILL PERFORM AT A HIGHER LEVEL, APPROACHING CHALLENGES WITH A POSITIVE MINDSET, MAKING MORE DECISIVE MOVES, AND STAYING RESILIENT UNDER PRESSURE. CONFIDENCE ALLOWS YOU TO FOCUS ON YOUR SKILLS AND STRENGTHS, LEADING TO IMPROVED PERFORMANCE, AND BETTER DECISION-MAKING. THIS BOOK WILL PROVIDE PRACTICAL TOOLS AND TECHNIQUES TO HELP YOU OVERCOME SELF-DOUBT, STAY MOTIVATED, AND PERFORM AT YOUR BEST, LEADING TO BETTER OUTCOMES AND MORE ENJOYMENT IN YOUR SPORT. A POSITIVE MINDSET EXTENDS BEYOND THE PLAYING FIELD OR COURT. BY CULTIVATING CONFIDENCE AND RESILIENCE YOU WILL DEVELOP SKILLS THAT WILL BENEFIT YOU IN ALL AREAS OF LIFE, FROM ACADEMICS TO CAREERS TO PERSONAL RELATIONSHIPS. THROUGH THE POWER OF A POSITIVE MINDSET, I HOPE YOU FIND THE MOTIVATION AND STRENGTH TO ACHIEVE YOUR GOALS.

TABLE OF CONTENTS

IF YOU ARE DIVING INTO THIS BOOK, IT IS PROBABLY BECAUSE YOU OR SOMEONE YOU KNOW IS GOING THROUGH A TOUGH TIME WITH THEIR SPORTS PERFORMANCE OR MENTAL MINDSET. WHETHER YOU ARE INTO BASKETBALL, SOCCER, FOOTBALL, VOLLEYBALL, CHEERLEADING, GYMNASTICS, TRACK, GOLF, LACROSSE, OR ANY OTHER SPORT, THIS BOOK IS YOUR KEY TO BOOSTING YOUR CONFIDENCE AND BREAKING FREE FROM THOSE MENTAL SHACKLES THAT ARE HOLDING YOU BACK. I HAVE BEEN THROUGH IT ALL: PLAYING BASKETBALL, SOFTBALL, RUNNING TRACK, AND CROSS-COUNTRY. I HAVE LEARNED THAT THE MENTAL GAME IS WHAT MATTERS MOST. EVEN WHEN I WAS NOT THE MOST SKILLFULLY PREPARED ATHLETE, I MANAGED TO COMPETE AT THE COLLEGE LEVEL BECAUSE MENTALLY, I WAS READY, I BELIEVED IN MYSELF. IT IS PROOF THAT ATHLETICS ARE 90% MENTAL AND ONLY 10% PHYSICAL SKILL. NOW, AS A PARENT SUPPORTING MY OWN YOUNG ATHLETE, I OBSERVE HER STRUGGLES WITH THE MENTAL SIDE OF THE GAME. SHE TRAINS EVERYDAY BUT I ASK, "WHY IS HER TRAINING NOT TRANSLATING INTO HER GAME PERFORMANCE?" THIS BOOK WILL HELP YOU SHIFT YOUR MINDSET AND TAKE YOUR GAME TO THE NEXT LEVEL. ARE YOU TRAINING HARD FOR HOURS EACH WEEK AND STILL NOT REACHING YOUR FULL POTENTIAL? YOU MAY HAVE THE PHYSICAL SKILLS; NOW, LET'S GET YOU MENTALLY PREPARED TO COMPETE AND WIN!

POSITIVE
THINKING IS KEY

ON MAY 7, 2002, BASKETBALL ICON ALLEN IVERSON
HELD A PRESS CONFERENCE. IVERSON SPOKE OF
HIS WINNING MINDSET AND HOW EFFORT WAS THE
KEY TO SUCCESS. IVERSON STATED THAT
WHEREVER HE GOES, HE WILL WIN. HE DID NOT
CARE WHICH TEAM HE PLAYED FOR, HE WAS GOING
TO WIN REGARDLESS. HE WAS CONFIDENT THAT HE
WOULD MAKE HIS TEAMMATES BETTER WHEREVER
HE WENT. IVERSON MENTIONED THAT HE HAD
BEEN IN THE LEAGUE FOR SIX YEARS AND FELT HE
HAD BEEN THE MVP FOR ALL SIX YEARS. HE
DECLARED THAT HE WOULD GO TO WAR FOR HIS
TEAM EVERY TIME THE JUMP BALL WAS THROWN
UP. IVERSON ACKNOWLEDGED THAT HE WOULD DO
SOME THINGS RIGHT AND SOME THINGS WRONG,
ADMITTING THAT HE WAS NOT GOING TO GET IT
RIGHT ALL THE TIME. HE REFERENCED MICHAEL

JORDAN AS THE GREATEST PLAYER IN THE WORLD, NOTING THAT EVEN JORDAN DIDN'T DO EVERYTHING RIGHT ALL THE TIME, BUT HE ALWAYS TRIED. JORDAN GAVE HIS BEST EFFORT, AND IVERSON EMPHASIZED THAT EFFORT IS ALL YOU CAN ASK FOR.

THIS TYPE OF POSITIVE THINKING IN SPORTS IS KEY BECAUSE IT IMPACTS YOUR OVERALL PERFORMANCE. POSITIVE THINKING HELPS YOU BELIEVE IN YOURSELF AND BOOSTS CONFIDENCE, WHICH, IN TURN, HELPS YOU STAY CALM UNDER PRESSURE AND TRUST IN YOUR SKILLS. HAVING A POSITIVE MINDSET WILL KEEP YOU FOCUSED AND SHIELD YOU FROM DISTRACTIONS. WHEN YOU THINK POSITIVELY, YOU STAY FOCUSED ON THE MOMENT RATHER THAN ON POSSIBLE MISTAKES OR OUTCOMES. YOU WIN SOME AND YOU LOSE SOME, HAVE GOOD GAMES AND BAD GAMES. POSITIVE THINKING HELPS YOU BOUNCE BACK FROM TOUGH LOSSES, TIME OUT DUE TO INJURIES, OR HAVING A BAD GAME. BASKETBALL LEGEND CHRIS BOSH SAID, *"LEGENDS ARE NOT DEFINED BY THEIR SUCCESSES. THEY'RE DEFINED BY HOW THEY BOUNCE BACK FROM THEIR FAILURES."* THIS QUOTE HIGHLIGHTS THAT TRUE GREATNESS IS NOT MEASURED BY BEING PERFECT BUT RATHER BY THE RESILIENCE AND DETERMINATION TO RISE AFTER YOU FALL. USE YOUR FAILURES AS FUEL FOR GROWTH, LEARNING FROM YOUR MISTAKES, AND USE EACH SETBACK AS A STEPPING STONE TO BECOME STRONGER.

POSITIVE THINKING WILL ALLOW YOU TO SEE MISTAKES OR FAILURES NOT AS A FINAL DEFEAT BUT AS A VALUABLE LESSON. RATHER THAN DWELLING ON WHAT WENT WRONG, FOCUS ON WHAT YOU CAN DO BETTER, MAINTAINING A FORWARD-LOOKING MINDSET. THIS ABILITY TO STAY POSITIVE AND RESILIENT IN THE FACE OF ADVERSITY IS WHAT WILL SET YOU APART.

HAVING A POSITIVE OUTLOOK WILL KEEP YOUR MOTIVATION AND DETERMINATION STRONG, LEADING TO BETTER PERFORMANCE. REPEATING POSITIVE THOUGHTS TO YOURSELF CAN INCREASE ENDURANCE AND STAMINA, HELPING YOU PUSH THROUGH MENTAL BLOCKAGES. THINKING POSITIVE ALSO HELPS TO CONTROL YOUR EMOTIONS. I OFTEN TELL MY DAUGHTER, *"CONTROL YOUR EMOTIONS, DON'T LET YOUR EMOTIONS CONTROL YOU."* THE ABILITY TO CONTROL YOUR EMOTIONS, HELPS REDUCE STRESS AND ANXIETY THAT CAN NEGATIVELY IMPACT YOUR PERFORMANCE. IT ALSO ALLOWS FOR MORE FUN DURING THE GAME, WHICH WILL PROVE TO BE CRUCIAL IN THE LONG-RUN. IF YOU WANT TO PLAY AT THE NEXT LEVEL, YOU HAVE TO LOVE WHAT YOU DO. FOR TEAM SPORTS, POSITIVITY IS VERY CONTAGIOUS. YOUR POSITIVE OUTLOOK CAN BOOST TEAM SPIRIT, ENHANCE COMMUNICATION, AND LEAD TO BETTER COLLABORATION ON AND OFF THE FIELD OR COURT.

KEEP UP THE POSITIVE THINKING AND YOU WILL START SEEING CHALLENGES AS AN OPPORTUNITY TO GROW; THIS WILL PROPEL YOU FORWARD IN YOUR TRAINING AND IN COMPETITION.

HERE IS SOMETHING YOU CAN PRACTICE: EVERY TIME YOU HAVE A NEGATIVE THOUGHT, TELL YOURSELF A POSITIVE, EMPOWERING STATEMENT CALLED AN AFFIRMATION. FOR EXAMPLE, AFFIRMATIONS LIKE "I AM GREAT AT MY SPORT" OR "I WILL ACHIEVE MY GOALS" CAN HELP YOU REFRAME YOUR MINDSET AND SHIFT BACK INTO POSITIVE THINKING. MY DAUGHTER STRUGGLED WITH SELF-DOUBT AFTER MAKING A MISTAKE. SHE NOW USES POSITIVE AFFIRMATIONS LIKE "I AM CAPABLE" TO QUICKLY BOUNCE BACK AND REFOCUS FOR THE NEXT PLAY, PREVENTING ONE MISTAKE FROM SNOWBALLING INTO A BAD GAME.

A POSITIVE MINDSET ALLOWS YOU TO NAVIGATE THE MENTAL SIDE OF SPORTS, KEEPING YOU FOCUSED, RESILIENT, AND ABLE TO ENJOY THE RIDE TOWARD YOUR PERSONAL BEST.

"I MISSED MORE THAN 9000 SHOTS IN MY CAREER. I'VE LOST ALMOST 300 GAMES. 26 TIMES I'VE BEEN TRUSTED TO TAKE THE GAME-WINNING SHOT AND MISSED, I'VE FAILED OVER AND OVER AND OVER AGAIN IN MY LIFE, AND THAT IS WHY I SUCCEEDED."

-MICHAEL JORDAN,
SIX-TIME NBA CHAMPION

MENTAL TRAINING WORKS

ON MY SPORTS JOURNEY, DEVELOPING MY MINDSET TOOK TIME. I FACED CHALLENGES EARLY ON THAT SHOWED ME HOW IMPORTANT MENTAL TOUGHNESS IS. THE SUMMER GOING INTO MY 10TH GRADE YEAR, I DID NOT MAKE THE AAU TEAM I TRIED OUT FOR. THIS PARTICULAR TEAM HAD A REPUTATION FOR BEING ONE OF THE BEST TEAMS IN MY AREA. WHEN SCHOOL STARTED AS A 10TH GRADER, I DID NOT MAKE THE VARSITY TEAM, WHILE TWO OF MY PEERS DID. THESE SETBACKS TURNED OUT TO BE A GAME-CHANGER. INSTEAD OF SEEING IT AS A FAILURE, I SAW IT AS A CHANCE TO LEARN AND GET BETTER. WITHOUT REALIZING IT, I STARTED ADDING MENTAL TRAINING TO MY ROUTINE, LIKE VISUALIZATION, MEDIATION, AND POSITIVE SELF-TALK. SETTING ACHIEVABLE GOALS BECAME A BIG PART OF SHAPING MY MINDSET.

EVERY LITTLE SUCCESS BOOSTED MY CONFIDENCE AND KEPT ME COMMITTED. I ENDED MY 10TH GRADE SEASON LEADING MY TEAM IN EVERY CATEGORY AND WAS AWARDED MVP. WHEN I WENT UP AGAINST TOUGH OPPONENTS, I STARTED SEEING PRESSURE AS A PRIVILEGE. TAKING ON CHALLENGES NOT ONLY MADE ME PERFORM BETTER BUT ALSO CHANGED HOW I SAW SETBACKS. FOR ME, AND HOPEFULLY YOU, SETBACKS WERE NOT ROADBLOCKS; THEY WERE STEPS TOWARD GETTING BETTER. PHYSICALLY, I DID NOT TRAIN A LOT, SIMPLY BECAUSE DURING MY ERA, TRAINING WAS NOT WIDELY AVAILABLE. THEREFORE, MENTALLY SHARPING MY MIND AND TOUGHNESS WAS KEY TO MY SUCCESS. IN RETROSPECT, HAD I POSSESSED THE PROPER TRAINING TO GO ALONG WITH MY MENTAL TOUGHNESS, I WOULD HAVE FAR SURPASSED MY ATHLETIC ACCOMPLISHMENTS. BOTH ARE IMPORTANT ELEMENTS, SO LET'S LOCK IN.

MENTAL TRAINING WORKS BECAUSE IT IMPROVES FOCUS, RESILIENCE, AND YOUR ABILITY TO MANAGE STRESS. THESE QUALITIES ARE ESSENTIAL FOR MAX PERFORMANCE. PHYSICAL SKILLS ARE IMPORTANT, BUT YOUR MINDSET CAN OFTEN BE THE DECIDING FACTOR IN CHALLENGING SITUATIONS. MENTAL TRAINING BUILDS A STRONG MENTAL FOUNDATION, SO YOU CAN APPROACH YOUR SPORT WITH CONFIDENCE, STAY FOCUSED, AND HANDLE SETBACKS EFFECTIVELY.

MENTAL TRAINING TEACHES YOU WAYS TO STAY FOCUSED, EVEN UNDER PRESSURE. TECHNIQUES LIKE MINDFULNESS, VISUALIZATION, AND CONTROLLED BREATHING WILL HELP YOU CONCENTRATE AND IGNORE DISTRACTIONS. RESILIENCE IS A MUST IN SPORTS, WHERE LOSSES, INJURIES, AND MISTAKES ARE GOING TO HAPPEN. MENTAL TRAINING STRESSES POSITIVE THINKING, SELF-COMPASSION, AND STRESS-MANAGEMENT, HELPING YOU STAY MENTALLY STRONG THROUGH TOUGH TIMES. YOU CAN USE AFFIRMATIONS AND VISUALIZATION TO BOOST YOUR CONFIDENCE AND PREPARE YOU FOR CHALLENGES. VISUALIZING POSITIVE OUTCOMES AND MENTALLY REHEARSING CHALLENGES CAN HELP YOU FEEL PREPARED. MENTAL TRAINING WILL MOTIVATE YOU TO SET AND ACHIEVE GOALS, GIVING YOU A CLEAR VISION OF WHAT YOU WANT TO ACCOMPLISH. WITH A CLEAR VISION, YOU ARE MORE LIKELY TO STAY COMMITTED TO TRAINING, EVEN WHEN FACED WITH SETBACKS. EMOTIONS CAN RUN HIGH DURING A GAME, LEADING TO MISTAKES IF NOT MANAGED PROPERLY. MENTAL TRAINING WILL PROVIDE YOU WITH TECHNIQUES LIKE DEEP BREATHING, PROGRESSIVE MUSCLE RELAXATION, AND MINDFULNESS TO CONTROL EMOTIONS AND STAY LEVEL-HEADED.

THIS BOOK WILL GIVE YOU THE TOOLS TO USE THE POWER OF YOUR MIND AS EFFECTIVELY AS YOUR BODY. THIS APPROACH ENSURES YOU ARE NOT

ONLY PHYSICALLY PREPARED BUT ALSO MENTALLY PREPARED TO HANDLE THE CHALLENGES OF THE GAME. PHIL JACKSON, AN 11-TIME NBA CHAMPION AND FORMER HEAD COACH OF THE LOS ANGELES LAKERS AND CHICAGO BULLS, COACHED LEGENDS LIKE KOBE BRYANT AND MICHAEL JORDAN. HE EMPHASIZED MINDFULNESS AS A CORE PART OF HIS COACHING PHILOSOPHY. HE BELIEVED THAT PLAYERS NEEDED TO DEVELOP MENTAL STRENGTH TO ACHIEVE SHARP FOCUS AND UNITY ON THE COURT. JACKSON OFTEN SPOKE ABOUT THE IMPORTANCE OF RESETTING THROUGH MINDFULNESS, ESPECIALLY IN MOMENTS OF ADVERSITY; WHETHER IT WAS A BAD CALL OR A TOUGH STRETCH IN THE GAME. HE ENCOURAGED HIS PLAYERS TO TAKE A DEEP BREATH, CENTER THEMSELVES, AND REGAIN FOCUS WHENEVER THEY CAME TO THE BENCH, ALLOWING THEM TO STAY PRESENT AND IN SYNC WITH THEIR TEAM. BY CENTERING THEMSELVES, PHIL JACKSON WANTED HIS PLAYERS TO CALM THEIR MINDS, REGAIN COMPOSURE, LET GO OF DISTRACTIONS OR STRESS, AND FOCUS ON THE PRESENT MOMENT.

A DEEP BREATHING TECHNIQUE YOU CAN USE IS CALLED "BOX BREATHING." TO PRACTICE IT, START BY INHALING DEEPLY THROUGH YOUR NOSE FOR 4 SECONDS, MAKING SURE TO FILL YOUR LUNGS COMPLETELY. HOLD YOUR BREATH FOR 4 SECONDS, KEEPING YOUR BODY RELAXED. THEN, EXHALE SLOWLY THROUGH YOUR MOUTH FOR 4 SECONDS,

LETTING GO OF ANY TENSION. FINALLY, PAUSE FOR ANOTHER 4 SECONDS BEFORE STARTING THE CYCLE AGAIN. YOU CAN REPEAT THIS 3-5 TIMES BEFORE A GAME, DURING A TIMEOUT, OR ANYTIME YOU NEED TO CALM YOUR NERVES AND REFOCUS.

"IF YOU WANT TO BE THE BEST, YOU HAVE TO DO THINGS THAT OTHER PEOPLE AREN'T WILLING TO DO."

-MICHAEL PHELPS,
23-TIME OLYMPIC GOLD MEDALIST

YOU ARE WHAT YOU THINK

PEOPLE BECOME WHAT THEY THINK ABOUT THEMSELVES. READ THAT AGAIN, PEOPLE BECOME WHAT THEY THINK ABOUT THEMSELVES. SO, TAKE SOME TIME TO UNDERSTAND YOUR THOUGHTS AND CHANGE THEM IN A POSITIVE WAY THAT HELPS YOU ACHIEVE YOUR DREAMS. THIS MEANS SETTING ASIDE TIME TO REFLECT ON WHAT YOU THINK AND FEEL. YOU CAN DO THIS BY WRITING IN A JOURNAL, MEDITATING, OR JUST TAKING QUIET MOMENTS TO THINK. BY DOING THIS, YOU CAN FIGURE OUT WHAT YOU TRULY BELIEVE ABOUT YOURSELF AND CHANGE ANY NEGATIVE THOUGHTS INTO POSITIVE ONES. THIS HELPS YOU BUILD CONFIDENCE AND A STRONG SENSE OF WHO YOU ARE AS A PERSON AND AS AN ATHLETE. WHEN YOU UNDERSTAND AND CONTROL YOUR THOUGHTS, YOU CAN BETTER SHAPE YOUR FUTURE AND BECOME THE PERSON YOU WANT TO BE.

YOU CAN NOT WORRY ABOUT WHAT OTHERS THINK ABOUT YOU. SUPER BOWL CHAMPION AND MLB PLAYER DEION SANDERS ONCE SAID IN AN INTERVIEW, *"DO NOT GIVE A DARN WHAT OPINIONS PEOPLE HAVE OF YOU, AS LONG AS THAT OPINION IS NOT CONSISTENT OF THAT OF YOURSELF, YOU BE YOU."* DEION'S STATEMENT EMPHASIZES THE IMPORTANCE OF STAYING TRUE TO YOURSELF, REGARDLESS OF OTHERS' PERCEPTIONS OR JUDGMENTS. STAY FOCUSED ON YOUR OWN SELF-WORTH AND IDENTITY RATHER THAN BEING INFLUENCED OR DEFINED BY EXTERNAL OPINIONS.

A FAMOUS HENRY FORD QUOTE STATES, *"WHETHER YOU THINK YOU CAN OR YOU THINK YOU CAN'T, YOU'RE RIGHT,"* EMPHASIZES, IF YOU THINK YOU ARE GOING TO FAIL, CHANCES ARE YOU WILL. IF YOU THINK YOU ARE GOING TO HAVE A GREAT GAME, GUESS WHAT? CHANCES ARE YOU WILL.

RESEARCH SHOWS THAT SOCIAL MEDIA PLATFORMS CAN MAKE SOCIAL COMPARISON WORSE, WHERE YOU COMPARE YOURSELF TO OTHERS, OFTEN LEADING TO NEGATIVE SELF EVALUATIONS AND INCREASED CONCERNS ABOUT OTHERS' OPINIONS OF YOU. I CAN NOT STRESS THIS ENOUGH: DO NOT WORRY ABOUT OTHERS' OPINIONS, IT IS A MAJOR CONFIDENCE BARRIER. INSTEAD OF SITTING THERE SCROLLING THROUGH YOUR PHONE OR WORKING ON THOSE SHIFTY SPORTS MOVES THAT YOU WON'T REGULARLY USE IN THE GAME,

TRY SOMETHING DIFFERENT. SPEND SOME TIME SITTING WITH YOUR OWN THOUGHTS. REMEMBER, JUST BEING GOOD AT FANCY MOVES DOES NOT MAKE YOU THE BEST PLAYER. THE ONES WHO FOCUS ON BOTH THEIR BODY AND THEIR MIND USUALLY DO BETTER IN THE GAME. SURE, IT'S FUN TO FLAUNT YOUR SKILLS AND SHOW OFF YOUR MOVES, BUT LET'S BE REAL, FANCY MOVES ALONE WILL ONLY GET YOU SO FAR, MAYBE STREETBALL LEGEND OR LOCAL STAR ATHLETE AT BEST. TAKE A LOOK AT COLLEGE BASKETBALL AS AN EXAMPLE. HOW MANY PLAYERS DO YOU SEE DOING FANCY MOVES? NOT MANY. ATHLETES ARE PLAYING IN A SYSTEM BUILT BY THEIR COACHES. COACHES ARE NOT HUNTING FOR FLASHY PLAYERS; THEY WANT SOMEONE WHO FITS INTO THEIR SYSTEM AND GETS THE JOB DONE. COACHES LOOK FOR PLAYERS WITH GREAT FUNDAMENTALS, GREAT FOOTWORK, A HIGH GAME IQ, INTENSITY, AND A POSITIVE ATTITUDE.

BELIEVE IT AND YOU WILL BECOME IT. HERE'S THE DEAL: IF YOU BELIEVE IN YOURSELF, YOU CAN MAKE IT HAPPEN. IF YOU ARE CONVINCED YOU'RE STUCK IN A SLUMP, WELL, GUESS WHAT? YOU WILL KEEP PLAYING LIKE YOU ARE STUCK IN THAT SLUMP. BUT IF YOU TRULY BELIEVE YOU ARE GOING TO HAVE A GREAT GAME, CHANCES ARE, YOU WILL. YOUR MINDSET CAN SHAPE YOUR PERFORMANCE. INDIVIDUALS TRANSFORM INTO A REFLECTION OF THEIR SELF-PERCEPTIONS.

SPEND MORE TIME EXPLORING HOW YOU CAN REWIRE YOUR THINKING HABITS IN A WAY THAT HELPS YOU REACH YOUR GOALS.

"EVERYBODY WANTS TO JUDGE, BUT NOBODY WANTS TO BE JUDGED."

-RED GRANT,
COMEDIAN AND HUMANITARIAN

THE IMPACT OF YOUR PEN

WRITING IN YOUR JOURNAL IS ONE WAY YOU CAN REFLECT ON WHAT YOU THINK AND FEEL. YOU CAN TRACK YOUR SPORTS PROGRESS, REFLECT ON YOUR MENTAL AND PHYSICAL PERFORMANCE, AND SET GOALS. AFTER EACH GAME OR PRACTICE, YOU SHOULD FOCUS ON KEY MOMENTS THAT STOOD OUT, WHETHER POSITIVE OR CHALLENGING, AND DESCRIBE HOW YOU FELT DURING THOSE MOMENTS. THIS INCLUDES EMOTIONS SUCH AS NERVOUSNESS, EXCITEMENT, OR FRUSTRATION, WHICH CAN HELP YOU BETTER UNDERSTAND YOUR MENTAL GAME. YOU SHOULD ALSO POINT OUT WHAT YOU DID WELL AND WHAT YOU NEED TO WORK ON, WHILE THINKING CAREFULLY ABOUT HOW YOU PLAYED. WRITING DOWN SHORT-TERM GOALS FOR THE NEXT GAME OR PRACTICE, AS WELL AS LONG-TERM GOALS, WILL KEEP YOU FOCUSED ON YOUR PROGRESS.

YOU SHOULD WRITE DOWN SPECIFIC STRENGTHS LIKE BALL-HANDLING OR COMMUNICATION, AS WELL AS AREAS THAT NEED WORK, SUCH AS FOOTWORK OR CONDITIONING. INCLUDE LESSONS LEARNED FROM EACH GAME, LIKE HOW YOU HANDLED PRESSURE, THIS WILL HELP YOU GROW. ADDING POSITIVE AFFIRMATIONS TO YOUR JOURNAL CAN HELP BOOST YOUR CONFIDENCE AND REMIND YOU TO STAY POSITIVE AFTER MAKING MISTAKES. IT IS IMPORTANT THAT YOU THINK ABOUT HOW YOU PREPARE FOR THE GAME, WHAT PREGAME ROUTINES OR HABITS HELP YOU PLAY WELL, AND ALSO HOW YOU WILL RECOVER OR GET BETTER AFTER THE GAME.

I CAME ACROSS AN ENTRY IN MY OLD HIGH SCHOOL SPORTS JOURNAL THAT I WOULD LIKE TO SHARE WITH YOU. I'VE MODIFIED IT SLIGHTLY TO FIT THIS BOOK. IT CAPTURES MY THOUGHTS AND FEELINGS ABOUT A GAME, HIGHLIGHTING KEY MOMENTS AND WHAT I LEARNED FROM THE EXPERIENCE. FINDING THIS JOURNAL AFTER SO MANY YEARS, WAS LIKE STEPPING INTO A TIME CAPSULE, FULL OF MEMORIES, EMOTIONS, AND REFLECTIONS FROM A YOUNGER VERSION OF MYSELF. IT BROUGHT BACK THE ADRENALINE OF GAMES, THE EXCITEMENT OF FRIENDSHIPS, AND A FRESH REMINDER OF HOW FAR I'VE COME SINCE THEN. AT THE END OF THIS BOOK, I'VE ADDED A FEW PAGES WITH THE HOPE THAT THEY WILL INSPIRE YOU TO START YOUR JOURNALING.

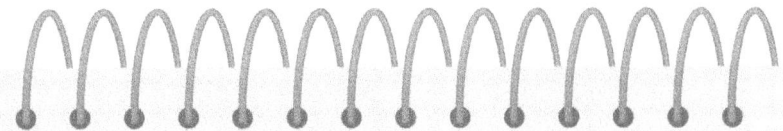

Sports Journal

1991-1992 SEASON
GAITHERSBURG HIGH SCHOOL VS. WATKINS MILL HIGH SCHOOL
MONTGOMERY COUNTY SEMIFINALS

TODAY'S GAME WAS CRAZY FROM THE JUMP. WITH A FEW SECONDS LEFT ON THE CLOCK, WE WERE UP BY ONE, AND I WAS GUARDING MARIA ACEVEDO. SHE CAUGHT THE BALL IN THE CORNER AND WENT UP FOR THE SHOT. I TRIED TO BLOCK IT, BUT I FOULED HER. ALL I COULD THINK ABOUT WAS I GAVE HER A CHANCE TO WIN THE GAME BY PUTTING HER ON THE FREE THROW LINE.. NEXT TIME I WILL CONTEST THE SHOT AND NOT TRY TO BLOCK IT.

MARIA WENT TO THE LINE, AND I WAS HOPING SO BADLY THAT SHE MISSED. THE FIRST SHOT WENT UP...AND SHE MISSED! I FELT A LITTLE BETTER BECAUSE NOW SHE COULD ONLY TIE THE GAME BUT I WAS STILL MAD AT MYSELF. COACH CALLED A TIMEOUT. I WALKED TO THE BENCH WITH MY HEAD DOWN. COACH JUST LOOKED AT ME AND SAID, "DON'T WORRY ABOUT IT,. STAY AGGRESSIVE AND FOCUS ON GETTING THE REBOUND." HE WASN'T MAD AT ME, MY TEAMMATES WEREN'T MAD AT ME, BUT I WAS SO MAD AT MYSELF. I NEEDED TO GET OVER IT BECAUSE THE GAME WASN'T OVER.

WHEN WE GOT BACK ON THE COURT, I KEPT TELLING MYSELF, "I'M GOING TO GET IT BACK, I'M GOING TO GET IT BACK." MARIA SHOT THE SECOND FREE THROW AND MISSED! THE CROWD EXPLODED. WE ULTIMATELY WON THE GAME. BUT I COULDN'T STOP THINKING ABOUT THAT FOUL.

AFTER THE GAME, COACH PULLED ME ASIDE AND REMINDED ME THAT ONE PLAY DOESN'T DEFINE A WHOLE GAME. BASKETBALL IS 32 MINUTES LONG, AND EVERY PLAY BUILDS ON THE NEXT. HE WAS RIGHT, AND I KNEW I HAD TO STOP THINKING ABOUT IT. I HAD TO FOCUS ON THE POSITIVES AND TRUST THAT I'M STILL LEARNING. MY OFFENSE WAS GOOD, I HIT SOME BIG SHOTS. WE PLAY SPRINGBROOK IN THE FINALS AND I KNOW I NEED TO STEP UP MY DEFENSE. TOMORROW AT PRACTICE, I'M GOING TO FOCUS ON MY FOOT SPEED AND ANTICIPATION SO I'M READY.

I'M LEARNING THAT I CAN'T GET STUCK ON ONE PLAY. I'VE GOT TO TRUST IN ME. I PUT ALL THAT PRESSURE ON MYSELF FOR NOTHING, FOR A FEAR THAT I CAUSED US TO LOSE THE GAME, AND WE WON.

BECOME A STUDENT

BECOMING A STUDENT OF A SPORT INVOLVES DEDICATING TIME. TO REALLY UNDERSTAND A SPORT, SPEND TIME GETTING TO KNOW ALL THE INS AND OUTS OF THAT SPORT. BECOME A STUDENT EXPERT OF YOUR SPORT. LEARN THE RULES; START WITH THE BASICS. GET A COPY OF THE OFFICIAL RULEBOOK FOR YOUR SPORT AND GO THROUGH IT THOROUGHLY. TALK TO REFEREES, THEY LOVE SHARING THEIR KNOWLEDGE OF THE GAME. UNDERSTANDING THE RULES IS FUNDAMENTAL TO PLAYING ANY SPORT.

OBSERVE THE WAY PLAYERS MOVE, AND WATCH BOTH COLLEGE AND PROFESSIONAL GAMES. I PREFER COLLEGE OVER PROFESSIONAL SPORTS FOR SEVERAL REASONS. COLLEGE SPORTS OFTEN STRESS PLAYER DEVELOPMENT AND TEAMWORK, SHOWCASING FUNDAMENTAL SKILLS AND STRATEGIES THAT ARE IMPORTANT FOR YOUNGER ATHLETES TO LEARN. COLLEGE TEAMS TEND TO SHOW A STRONG SENSE OF FRIENDSHIP AND

TEAMWORK, HIGHLIGHTING THE VALUE OF WORKING TOGETHER AND SUPPORT AMONG TEAMMATES. THE COLLEGE GAME IS OFTEN EASIER TO UNDERSTAND, ALLOWING YOU TO EASILY UNDERSTAND THE FUNDAMENTALS. THE COMPETITIVE NATURE OF COLLEGE SPORTS SHOWS THE IMPORTANCE OF HARD WORK, DEDICATION AND RESILIENCE. WATCHING COLLEGE SPORTS CAN INSPIRE YOU TO PURSUE YOUR OWN ATHLETIC GOALS, PROVIDING A REALISTIC GLIMPSE INTO WHAT YOU CAN ASPIRE TO ACHIEVE.

OBSERVING HOW OTHERS PLAY CAN PROVIDE INSIGHTS INTO THE RULES IN ACTION AND HELP YOU UNDERSTAND DIFFERENT STRATEGIES AND TACTICS. IT CAN ALSO HELP YOU MIMIC MOVEMENTS OF GREAT PLAYERS. LOOK AT HOW SIMILAR KOBE BRYANT AND MICHAEL JORDAN PLAYED. IT IS OBVIOUS THAT KOBE STUDIED MICHAEL'S MOVEMENTS AND PERFECTED THEM AS HIS OWN. REFERRING TO MICHAEL JORDAN, KOBE IS QUOTED AS SAYING, *"I DON'T THINK PEOPLE REALLY UNDERSTAND THE AMOUNT OF IMPACT HE'S HAD ON ME AS A PLAYER AND AS A LEADER."* SEEK ADVICE FROM MORE EXPERIENCED PLAYERS. THEY HAVE VALUABLE INSIGHTS INTO THE NUANCES OF THE GAME, STRATEGIES THAT WORK, AND HOW TO NAVIGATE VARIOUS SITUATIONS. HAVE SOMEONE FILM YOUR GAMES.

AFTER EACH GAME, TAKE A MOMENT TO CHECK OUT YOUR GAME FOOTAGE. THIS WILL ALLOW YOU TO EVALUATE YOURSELF, IDENTIFYING STRENGTHS AND WEAKNESSES IN YOUR SKILLS AND DECISION-MAKING. BY STUDYING GAME FILM, YOU CAN SEE WHAT WORKED WELL AND WHAT DIDN'T, HELPING YOU MAKE NECESSARY ADJUSTMENTS IN PRACTICE AND FUTURE GAMES. STUDYING YOUR GAME PERFORMANCE IS KEY TO BECOMING A TOP-NOTCH STUDENT OF THE GAME. STUDYING YOUR OPPONENTS IS EQUALLY IMPORTANT. BY LOOKING AT THEIR GAME FOOTAGE, YOU CAN UNDERSTAND THEIR PLAYING STYLE, STRENGTHS, AND WEAKNESSES. UNDERSTANDING YOUR OPPONENTS' STRATEGIES ALLOWS YOU TO ANTICIPATE THEIR MOVES AND DEVELOP EFFECTIVE GAME PLANS. IN SCHOOL AND AAU, YOU OFTEN COMPETE AGAINST THE SAME PLAYERS. IF YOU PAY ATTENTION TO HOW THEY PLAY AND STUDY THEIR MOVES, YOU WILL START TO UNDERSTAND THEIR GAME. THIS KNOWLEDGE CAN HELP YOU TAKE ADVANTAGE OF THEIR WEAKNESSES AND PREPARE YOU TO DEFEND AGAINST THEIR STRENGTHS.

REVIEWING YOUR OWN FOOTAGE AND STUDYING YOUR OPPONENTS PROVIDES A BETTER UNDERSTANDING OF THE GAME, HELPING YOU EVALUATE YOUR PERFORMANCE ON BOTH DEFENSE AND OFFENSE. KEEP A MINDSET OF ALWAYS LEARNING, WHETHER IT'S FROM READING,

WATCHING GAMES, OR ACTUALLY PLAYING, SO YOU CAN GET BETTER AND BETTER AS YOU GO. REMEMBER, UNDERSTANDING THE RULES, STRATEGIES, AND TACTICS IS AN ONGOING PROCESS. KEEP UP WITH WHAT IS NEW IN YOUR SPORT. STAY CURIOUS, BE OPEN TO LEARNING FROM VARIOUS SOURCES, AND ENJOY THE JOURNEY OF IMPROVING YOUR MINDSET AND SKILLS IN YOUR SPORT.

TRY NEW THINGS

LET'S MAKE THIS CLEAR, CLAIMING YOU ARE A GREAT PLAYER WILL NOT MAKE YOU ONE AUTOMATICALLY. ACHIEVING GREATNESS REQUIRES INCREDIBLE PHYSICAL SKILLS AND MENTAL EFFORTS. EMBRACE NEW CHALLENGES AND FACE YOUR FEARS HEAD-ON. CONFIDENCE GROWS WHEN YOU DO. REPROGRAM YOUR MIND BY TACKLING WHAT SCARES YOU. YOU HAVE TO PUT IN THE WORK PHYSICALLY AND MENTALLY. PRACTICE BOTH CONSISTENTLY; EACH REPETITION BOOSTS YOUR CONFIDENCE.

THE MORE YOU DO SOMETHING, THE MORE CONFIDENT YOU FEEL DOING IT. I ONCE HEARD A QUOTE BY JOHN FLANAGAN THAT GOES, "*DON'T PRACTICE UNTIL YOU GET IT RIGHT; PRACTICE UNTIL YOU NEVER GET IT WRONG.*" THIS WILL BUILD MUSCLE MEMORY, SO YOUR MOVES, SHOT, SWINGS, OR SWIM STROKE WILL HAPPEN WITHOUT THOUGHT. YOUR TRAINING SHOULD BE A CARBON COPY OF WHAT YOU ARE DOING IN THE GAME. APPROACH EACH TRAINING SESSION WITH A PLAN, WHAT PASSING ROUTES, SHOTS, OR MOVES DO YOU TAKE IN THE GAME? HOW CAN YOU ATTACK THIS IN A WAY THAT LETS YOU TRACK YOUR PROGRESS? BE MORE TARGETED AND ORGANIZED, SET GOALS YOU CAN REACH. YOUR BODY IMPACTS YOUR MIND; AFTER EACH PRACTICE, YOUR BRAIN SIGNALS A SENSE OF ACHIEVEMENT, WHICH BOOSTS YOUR CONFIDENCE AND REINFORCES A POSITIVE MINDSET.

YOU KNOW THAT MOVE YOU CAN DO IN PRACTICE BUT ARE SCARED TO USE IN A GAME BECAUSE YOU MIGHT MESS UP? TRY IT ANYWAY. YOU MIGHT MESS UP THE FIRST FEW TIMES, BUT MASTERING IT IS THE GOAL. PEOPLE MAY LAUGH AT YOU, BUT THEY WILL PRAISE YOUR GREATNESS WHEN YOU KEEP GOING DESPITE FAILURES. DO NOT FEAR MISTAKES, SUCCESS COMES THROUGH PERSISTENCE. ONCE YOU HAVE IT DOWN, NO ONE WILL REMEMBER THE TIMES YOU MESSED UP. THEY WILL ONLY REMEMBER HOW

AWESOME THE MOVE IS NOW. FOCUS ON THE END GOAL, AND THAT IS WHAT WILL MAKE YOU GREAT. GREAT PLAYERS DO NOT BECOME GREAT BECAUSE THEY ARE SCARED TO TRY NEW MOVES. NO, THEY BECOME GREAT BECAUSE THEY HAVE TRIED AND FAILED AND TRIED AGAIN.

EMBRACE MINDFULLNESS

MINDFULNESS IS ABOUT STAYING COMPLETELY FOCUSED ON THE PRESENT MOMENT, WITHOUT PASSING JUDGMENT. IT MEANS BEING AWARE OF YOUR THOUGHTS, FEELINGS, AND WHAT IS HAPPENING AROUND YOU, HELPING YOU FEEL CLEAR-HEADED, FOCUSED, AND CALM.

TO BE MINDFUL IN SPORTS, BEGIN BY TAKING A DEEP BREATH AND PAYING ATTENTION TO THINGS LIKE HOW THE BALL, STICK, OR CLUB FEELS, YOUR BODY MOVEMENTS, AND THE SOUNDS AROUND YOU. IF YOUR MIND WANDERS, GENTLY BRING IT BACK. TRY SHORT MEDITATION SESSIONS AND IMAGINE DOING GREAT IN YOUR GAME OR COMPETITION.

PRACTICING THIS REGULARLY WILL HELP YOU CONCENTRATE BETTER, MAKE SMARTER CHOICES, AND MAKE PLAYING YOUR SPORT EVEN MORE FUN.

LET'S PRACTICE MEDITATION

CLOSE YOUR EYES AND TAKE A FEW DEEP BREATHS, INHALING SLOWLY THROUGH YOUR NOSE AND EXHALING THROUGH YOUR MOUTH. BEGIN TO FOCUS ON YOUR BREATHING, NOTICING EACH INHALE AND EXHALE, LETTING GO OF ANY THOUGHTS OR WORRIES ABOUT YOUR PERFORMANCE. WHEN YOUR MIND WANDERS, GENTLY BRING YOUR FOCUS BACK TO YOUR BREATH. AS YOU SETTLE INTO THIS RHYTHM, VISUALIZE YOURSELF IN A GAME OR PRACTICE, STAYING CALM AND CENTERED. PICTURE YOURSELF EXECUTING PLAYS WITH FOCUS AND CONFIDENCE, SEEING EACH MOVEMENT CLEARLY IN YOUR MIND. THIS MENTAL REHEARSAL HELPS YOU STAY COMPOSED UNDER PRESSURE, MAKING IT EASIER TO STAY IN THE MOMENT DURING COMPETITION. WITH REGULAR PRACTICE, MEDITATION CAN TRAIN YOUR MIND TO BE MORE RESILIENT, HELPING YOU TO RESPOND CALMLY TO CHALLENGES AND BOOST YOUR OVERALL MENTAL STRENGTH ON AND OFF THE FIELD OR COURT.

DURING YOUR TRAINING, YOU ARE HITTING MOST OF YOUR SHOTS, CATCHING ALL OF THE BALLS, OR SCORING GOALS, SO WHY ARE YOU HAVING DIFFERENT RESULTS IN THE GAME? THE BALL DOES NOT CHANGE, THE BASKET DOES NOT CHANGE, THE ONLY THING THAT CHANGES IS YOUR MINDSET.

DO YOUR PARENTS OR COACHES EVER TELL YOU, "YOU'RE IN YOUR HEAD," OR, "GET OUT OF YOUR HEAD"? WHAT DOES THAT MEAN? THEY MEAN THAT YOU ARE OVERTHINKING OR LETTING YOUR MENTAL STATE AFFECT YOUR PERFORMANCE. THIS CAN INCLUDE FEELING NERVOUS, DOUBTING YOUR ABILITIES, OR FOCUSING TOO MUCH ON THE OUTCOME RATHER THAN THE PROCESS. THESE MENTAL BARRIERS CAN HINDER YOUR NATURAL PERFORMANCE, CAUSING YOU TO MAKE ERRORS THAT YOU WOULD NORMALLY NOT MAKE DURING PRACTICE. BY EMBRACING AND IMPLEMENTING MINDFULNESS, YOU CAN OVERCOME THESE BARRIERS.

PRIOR TO EVERY GAME, TELL YOURSELF THAT YOU WILL HAVE A GREAT GAME, SCORE MORE, RUN FASTER, LAND THE PERFECT MOVE, OR BE THE BEST DEFENDER. CONVINCE YOURSELF OF YOUR GAME GOALS. SELF-CONFIDENCE THRIVES ON RECOGNIZING YOUR TALENTS. REMIND YOURSELF DAILY OF YOUR STRENGTHS TO BOOST SELF-ESTEEM. YOU CAN START BY WRITING

AFFIRMATIONS LIKE, "I AM A STRONG ATHLETE" OR "I EXCEL UNDER PRESSURE" AND REPEAT THEM EACH MORNING. KEEP A JOURNAL OF YOUR TRAINING MILESTONES, GAME HIGHLIGHTS, AND PERSONAL BESTS TO TRACK YOUR PROGRESS AND SEE HOW FAR YOU HAVE COME. PLACE MOTIVATIONAL QUOTES FROM YOUR FAVORITE ATHLETES OR YOUR OWN ENCOURAGING MESSAGES IN YOUR LOCKER, BEDROOM, GYM BAG, OR TRAINING AREA AS VISUAL REMINDERS.

IN AN INTERVIEW I CAME ACROSS ON INSTAGRAM, OLYMPIC GOLD MEDALIST GABBY THOMAS SHARED THAT SHE BUILT HER SELF-TALK AND SELF-CONFIDENCE BY TELLING HERSELF, IN THE MOMENT JUST BEFORE THE RACE, THAT SHE WAS ALREADY THE OLYMPIC CHAMPION. EVERY MORNING IN PARIS, SHE WROTE DOWN REPEATEDLY, "I WILL BE THE OLYMPIC CHAMPION." GABBY ENVISIONED THE RACE ALL DAY, EVERY DAY, IMAGINING HERSELF WINNING AND CROSSING THE FINISH LINE FIRST. FOR HER, PREPARATION WAS KEY. SHE KNEW SHE WAS UP AGAINST AMAZING ATHLETES AND THE REIGNING OLYMPIC CHAMPION, WHO HAD WON JUST A FEW DAYS PRIOR. GABBY STATED THAT SHE HAD YEARS OF PRACTICE, TRAINING, AND MUSCLE MEMORY ON HER SIDE. SHE KNEW SHE WAS READY FOR THAT MOMENT, AND THAT WAS ALL SHE NEEDED TO KNOW. SIMONE BILES, AN OLYMPIC GYMNAST, TAKES A DEEP BREATH BEFORE HER ROUTINE AND

SAYS, "I GOT THIS." THIS SIMPLE ACT HELPS HER RELIEVE STRESS AND PUSH AWAY NEGATIVE THOUGHTS. THESE ARE GREAT EXAMPLES OF HOW OUR THOUGHTS INFLUENCE OUR ACTIONS. WHEN WE FILL OUR MINDS WITH POSITIVE, EMPOWERING MESSAGES, WE SET OURSELVES UP FOR SUCCESS. ON THE OTHER HAND, NEGATIVE THOUGHTS CAN HOLD US BACK, CREATING FEAR AND HESITATION. THIS SHOWS US THAT EVEN THE MOST SUCCESSFUL ATHLETES RELY ON SIMPLE MENTAL STRATEGIES TO STAY FOCUSED AND CONFIDENT. REFLECT ON ASPECTS OF YOUR SPORTS JOURNEY YOU ARE GRATEFUL FOR, SUCH AS SKILLS YOU HAVE MASTERED OR SUPPORTIVE TEAMMATES AND COACHES. CREATE AND ACCOMPLISH SMALL, ACHIEVABLE GOALS EACH DAY, LIKE IMPROVING A SPECIFIC SKILL OR COMPLETING A WORKOUT, TO BUILD A SENSE OF ACHIEVEMENT. INCORPORATE SELF-CARE PRACTICES SUCH AS STRETCHING, PROPER NUTRITION, AND REST TO KEEP YOUR BODY AND MIND IN TOP SHAPE. LASTLY, SURROUND YOURSELF WITH SUPPORTIVE TEAMMATES, COACHES, AND FRIENDS WHO UPLIFT AND MOTIVATE YOU. AUTHOR AND MOTIVATIONAL SPEAKER JIM ROHN SAID, *"IF YOU HANG AROUND WITH THREE MILLIONAIRES, YOU WILL BECOME THE FOURTH."* THE INFLUENCE OF WHO YOU ASSOCIATE AND HANG WITH CAN DIRECTLY IMPACT YOUR SUCCESS AND MINDSET. FIND FRIENDS, INFLUENCERS, AND MENTORS THAT HAVE THE SAME OR SIMILAR GOALS AS YOU.

THIS APPROACH WILL HELP YOU CONSISTENTLY RECOGNIZE AND REINFORCE YOUR STRENGTHS, BOOSTING YOUR CONFIDENCE IN SPORTS.

PRACTICING MINDFULNESS IN SPORTS IS CRUCIAL BECAUSE IT BOOSTS YOUR CONCENTRATION, DECISION-MAKING, AND PERFORMANCE. IT ASSISTS IN STAYING IN THE MOMENT, HANDLING STRESS, AND TACKLING CHALLENGES EFFECTIVELY. MINDFULNESS ALSO MAKES YOU MORE AWARE OF YOUR BODY MOVEMENTS, MAKING YOU MORE COORDINATED AND PRECISE. PRACTICING MINDFULNESS WILL MAKE YOUR SPORTS EXPERIENCE MORE ENJOYABLE AND SATISFYING, WHILE ALSO BUILDING MENTAL STRENGTH.

"YOU DON'T ALWAYS HAVE TO BE DOING SOMETHING. YOU CAN JUST BREATHE, TAKE A MOMENT, AND ENJOY THE STILLNESS."

-ALY RAISMAN,
OLYMPIC GOLD MEDALIST

VISUALIZE YOUR PERFORMANCE

VISUALIZING IS LIKE A MENTAL JUMP START FOR YOUR GAME. YOU CAN DO IT IN A QUIET SPOT, OR EVEN WHILE YOU ARE HEADING TO A GAME. YOU CAN HAVE YOUR HEADPHONES ON OR OFF, LYING DOWN OR SITTING UP, EYES OPEN OR CLOSED; WHATEVER MAKES YOU COMFORTABLE.

VISUALIZATION IS THE PRACTICE OF CREATING A MENTAL IMAGE OF YOURSELF ACHIEVING A GOAL OR PERFORMING AT YOUR BEST. IT'S LIKE IMAGINING A MOVIE IN YOUR MIND WHERE YOU SEE YOURSELF SUCCEEDING, WHETHER IT'S SCORING THE WINNING TOUCHDOWN, HAVING A GREAT GAME, OR OVERCOMING A CHALLENGE. BY PICTURING IT CLEARLY AND IN DETAIL, YOU CAN BUILD CONFIDENCE, STAY FOCUSED, AND PREPARE YOUR MIND AND BODY TO MAKE IT HAPPEN IN REAL LIFE.

VISUALIZE BEFORE EACH GAME; IT GETS EASIER AND MORE EFFECTIVE THE MORE YOU DO IT. PICTURE NAILING SPECIFIC GOALS, LIKE MAKING THE PERFECT SHOT, PULLING OFF A GREAT MOVE OR HITTING A HOME RUN. FOCUS ON THE GOOD STUFF, NOT ON AVOIDING MISTAKES. TECHNIQUES LIKE MINDFULNESS, VISUALIZATION, AND CONTROLLED BREATHING WILL ALLOW YOU TO CONCENTRATE ON EACH MOMENT AND FILTER OUT DISTRACTIONS. IMAGINE YOURSELF STEPPING UP TO THE PLATE WITH CONFIDENCE, FEELING THE BAT'S WEIGHT IN YOUR HANDS, WATCHING THE PERFECT PITCH APPROACH, THEN SWINGING SMOOTHLY, MAKING SOLID CONTACT, AND SEEING THE BALL SOAR OVER THE OUTFIELD FENCE AS YOU ROUND THE BASES WITH EASE AND EXCITEMENT. PICTURE YOURSELF SPRINTING DOWN THE FIELD, MAKING EYE CONTACT WITH THE QUARTERBACK AS THE BALL ARCS THROUGH THE AIR, EXTENDING YOUR HANDS AT THE PERFECT MOMENT, FEELING THE BALL LAND SECURELY IN YOUR HANDS, THEN CROSSING THE GOAL LINE WITH CONTROL AND CONFIDENCE AS THE CROWD ERUPTS IN CELEBRATION. USE VISUALIZATION TO MENTALLY PRACTICE FREE THROWS, IMAGINING EACH SHOT GOING IN. WHEN YOU STEP TO THE LINE, YOU'RE MORE LIKELY TO FOCUS FULLY ON YOUR TECHNIQUE RATHER THAN FEELING ANXIOUS ABOUT THE OUTCOME.

VISUALIZATION EXERCISE

LET'S PRACTICE USING VISUALIZATION TO HELP MENTALLY PREPARE FOR GAMES OR PRACTICE.

TAKE SOME DEEP BREATHS, AND PICTURE YOURSELF TOTALLY KILLING IT IN YOUR SPORT. IMAGINE ALL THE DETAILS: WHERE YOU ARE, WHAT YOU ARE DOING, WHAT YOU ARE SEEING, AND WHAT YOU ARE SMELLING,

TRY TO FEEL THE TEXTURES, HEAR THE SOUNDS, AND REALLY GET INTO THE MOMENT LIKE YOU ARE ACTUALLY PLAYING. LET YOURSELF FEEL THE GREAT ENERGY, WHETHER IT IS JOY, CONFIDENCE, OR EXCITEMENT.

NOW IMAGINE THE AMAZING RESULTS: HITTING THE GAME WINNING SHOT, CATCHING A TOUCHDOWN, HITTING A HOME RUN, WINNING THE RACE, SCORING A GOAL, NOT TURNING THE BALL OVER UNDER PRESSURE, STAYING CALM UNDER PRESSURE, OR MAKING YOUR FREE THROWS.

POSITIVE VISUALIZATION BOOSTS YOUR CONFIDENCE AND PERFORMANCE. KEEP AT IT, AND SOON IT WILL BE PART OF YOUR ROUTINE.

"VISUALIZING AND MENTAL PREPARATION IS EVERY BIT AS EFFECTIVE AS PHYSICAL PREPARATION."
-PHIL MICKELSON,
THREE-TIME MASTERS CHAMPION

REALITY IS REAL

DO NOT LIVE IN A FEAR-BASED MINDSET WHERE YOUR REALITY IS BASED ON A FEAR OF SOMETHING THAT HAS NOT HAPPENED. FOR EXAMPLE, YOU ARE GOING TO HAVE A BAD GAME, SOMEONE IS GOING TO MAKE A MOVE AND EMBARRASS YOU OR YOU ARE GOING TO MISS A SHOT. APPROACH THE GAME WITH A POSITIVE-BASED MINDSET, WHERE YOUR PERSPECTIVE IS BASED ON ACTUAL GREAT GAMES YOU HAVE PLAYED, GREAT SHOTS YOU HAVE MADE, OR GREAT MOVES YOU HAVE MASTERED. YOUR FEARS ARE NOT REAL AND WILL NEGATIVELY IMPACT THE WAY YOU PLAY. FEAR IS AN EMOTION OF SOMETHING THAT DOES NOT EXIST. IMAGINE WHAT YOU CAN DO ONCE YOU GET OVER YOUR FEAR. MARK TWAIN IS QUOTED AS SAYING, "*I'VE HAD A LOT OF WORRIES IN MY LIFE, MOST OF WHICH NEVER HAPPENED.*"

MOST OF THE TIME, WE PUT OURSELVES UNDER A LOT OF PRESSURE—PRESSURE THAT DOES NOT ACTUALLY EXIST, BUT THAT WE CREATE OURSELVES. WE BUILD UP TENSION AND ANXIETY OVER THINGS THAT ARE NOT REAL. WHEN YOU FEEL FEAR AND ANXIETY, DO YOU PERFORM BETTER OR WORSE? WORSE. FOR EXAMPLE, YOU STEP UP TO THE FREE THROW LINE WITH ALL THIS TENSION AND ANXIETY THAT YOU CREATED BECAUSE YOU ARE WORRIED ABOUT MISSING THE SHOT —AND GUESS WHAT? YOU MISS. THE VERY THING YOU WERE AFRAID OF HAPPENS. THIS SHOWS HOW POWERFUL A NEGATIVE MINDSET CAN BE AND WHY IT IS SO IMPORTANT TO FOCUS ON BUILDING A POSITIVE ONE. LET'S WORK ON CREATING A POSITIVE MINDSET.

THIS INTERNAL PRESSURE CAN LEAD TO HEIGHTENED ANXIETY, CAUSING YOU TO SECOND-GUESS YOUR ABILITIES AND BECOME OVERLY FOCUSED ON THE POSSIBILITY OF FAILURE RATHER THAN ON THE JOY OF THE GAME. WHEN FEAR DOMINATES YOUR THOUGHTS, YOU MAY AVOID TAKING RISKS, HOLDING BACK YOUR CREATIVITY. A FEAR-BASED MINDSET CAN CREATE A NEGATIVE FEEDBACK LOOP, WHERE THE FEAR OF MAKING MISTAKES LEADS TO MISTAKES. ASK YOURSELF, "ARE YOU PLAYING TO GET BETTER OR PLAYING TO NOT MAKE A MISTAKE?" HOPEFULLY YOU ARE PLAYING TO LEARN, TO FIGURE THINGS

OUT, AND ULTIMATELY GET BETTER. IF YOU STAY IN THAT NEGATIVE FEEDBACK LOOP, YOU CAN LOSE YOUR CONFIDENCE AND LOVE OF THE SPORT, MAKING IT HARD TO PLAY YOUR BEST AND STOPPING YOUR GROWTH AS AN ATHLETE. TAKING ON A MORE POSITIVE, GROWTH-ORIENTED MINDSET, CAN HELP YOU OVERCOME THESE CHALLENGES, ALLOWING YOU TO THRIVE WHEN THE COMPETITION GETS TOUGH. HERE ARE SEVERAL THINGS YOU CAN DO TO OVERCOME A FEAR-BASED MINDSET AND DEVELOP A MORE POSITIVE, PERFORMANCE-ENHANCING MINDSET.

- SETTING REALISTIC GOALS WILL ALLOW YOU TO FOCUS ON THE PROCESS RATHER THAN THE OUTCOME, BREAKING BIG GOALS INTO SMALLER GOALS AND CELEBRATING EACH SMALL SUCCESS.
- ACCEPTING MISTAKES AS LEARNING OPPORTUNITIES, THIS WILL ALLOW YOU TO VIEW ERRORS AS CHANCES TO GET BETTER RATHER THAN FAILURES.
- DEVELOPING A CONSISTENT PRE-GAME ROUTINE, WHICH MIGHT INCLUDE RELAXATION TECHNIQUES, BREATHING EXERCISES, OR POSITIVE SELF-TALK CAN HELP MANAGE ANXIETY AND ENHANCE FOCUS.
- SIT DOWN AND VISUALIZE HOW YOU SEE YOURSELF. TAKE THAT PICTURE IN YOUR HEAD AND WRITE IT OUT: "I SEE MYSELF AS....." READ IT OVER AND OVER AGAIN. IT MAY BE A FANTASY AT FIRST, BUT EVENTUALLY, YOU WILL START TO BELIEVE IT. WHAT WE BELIEVE, WE BECOME.

PRACTICING MINDFULNESS WILL HELP YOU CONCENTRATE ON THE PRESENT MOMENT, REDUCING WORRIES ABOUT PAST MISTAKES OR FUTURE OUTCOMES.

BECOME A BETTER ATHLETE

GETTING YOUR MINDSET RIGHT CAN BE TOUGH, BUT THERE ARE THINGS YOU CAN DO TO HELP. ONCE YOU HAVE ENHANCED YOUR ATHLETIC SKILLS AND PHYSICAL FITNESS, TRAINING YOUR MIND BECOMES A BIT EASIER. HERE ARE 7 THINGS YOU CAN WORK ON TO HELP YOU ELEVATE YOUR GAME.

1. TRAIN CONSISTENTLY:

MAKE SURE YOU ARE REGULARLY WORKING OUT WITH A GOOD MIX. BUILD STRENGTH, AGILITY, AND ENDURANCE. FOCUS ON GETTING BETTER AT THE SKILLS YOU NEED FOR YOUR SPORT.

2. BE A GOAL GETTER:

SET SHORT TERM AND LONG TERM GOALS. IT GIVES YOU A PATH TO FOLLOW AND KEEPS YOU MOTIVATED DURING YOUR TRAINING, LETTING YOU SEE HOW FAR YOU HAVE COME AND WHAT YOU NEED TO LOOK FORWARD TO. IF YOU ARE A SOCCER PLAYER FOR INSTANCE, SET SPECIFIC, MEASURABLE GOALS, LIKE INCREASING SHOT ACCURACY OR SPEED. MAKING EACH TRAINING SESSION PURPOSEFUL, SHORT-TERM GOALS WILL KEEP YOU MOTIVATED TOWARD YOUR LONG-TERM ACHIEVEMENTS.

3. NUTRITION IS KEY:

EAT A BALANCED AND HEALTHY DIET TO KEEP YOUR ENERGY UP, HELP YOUR BODY RECOVER, AND BOOST YOUR OVERALL PERFORMANCE. MY ADVICE WOULD BE TO EAT A WELL BALANCED DIET OF MEATS, VEGETABLES, FRUIT, LEGUMES (BEANS) AND GRAINS. TAKE A LOOK AT THE FOOD CHART IN THIS BOOK AND SEE THE BENEFITS OF EACH FOOD GROUP. IF YOU NEED ADVICE, CONSIDER TALKING TO A NUTRITIONIST.

4. REST AND RECOVERY:

GIVE YOUR BODY THE TIME IT NEEDS TO RECOVER. GOOD SLEEP (8-9 HOURS A NIGHT), TAKING REST DAYS, AND USING APPROPRIATE RECOVERY METHODS ARE SUPER IMPORTANT TO PREVENT BURNOUT AND INJURIES. STRETCH BEFORE AND AFTER PRACTICE. STRETCHING IMPROVES FLEXIBILITY, INCREASES RANGE OF MOTION, AND MAY HELP PREVENT INJURIES BY ENHANCING BETTER MUSCLE FUNCTION AND JOINT MOBILITY. CONSIDER ICING AFTER A WORKOUT. ICING HELPS REDUCE INFLAMMATION AND MUSCLE SORENESS. IT CAN ALSO HELP IN MINIMIZING SWELLING AND SPEEDING UP THE RECOVERY PROCESS.

5. CONSISTENT EVALUATION:

TAKE NOTE ON WHAT YOU ARE DOING WELL AND WHERE YOU CAN GET BETTER. ADJUST YOUR TRAINING ROUTINE TO FOCUS ON IMPROVING THE AREAS THAT NEED IMPROVEMENT. MASTER THAT AREA BEFORE MOVING ON.

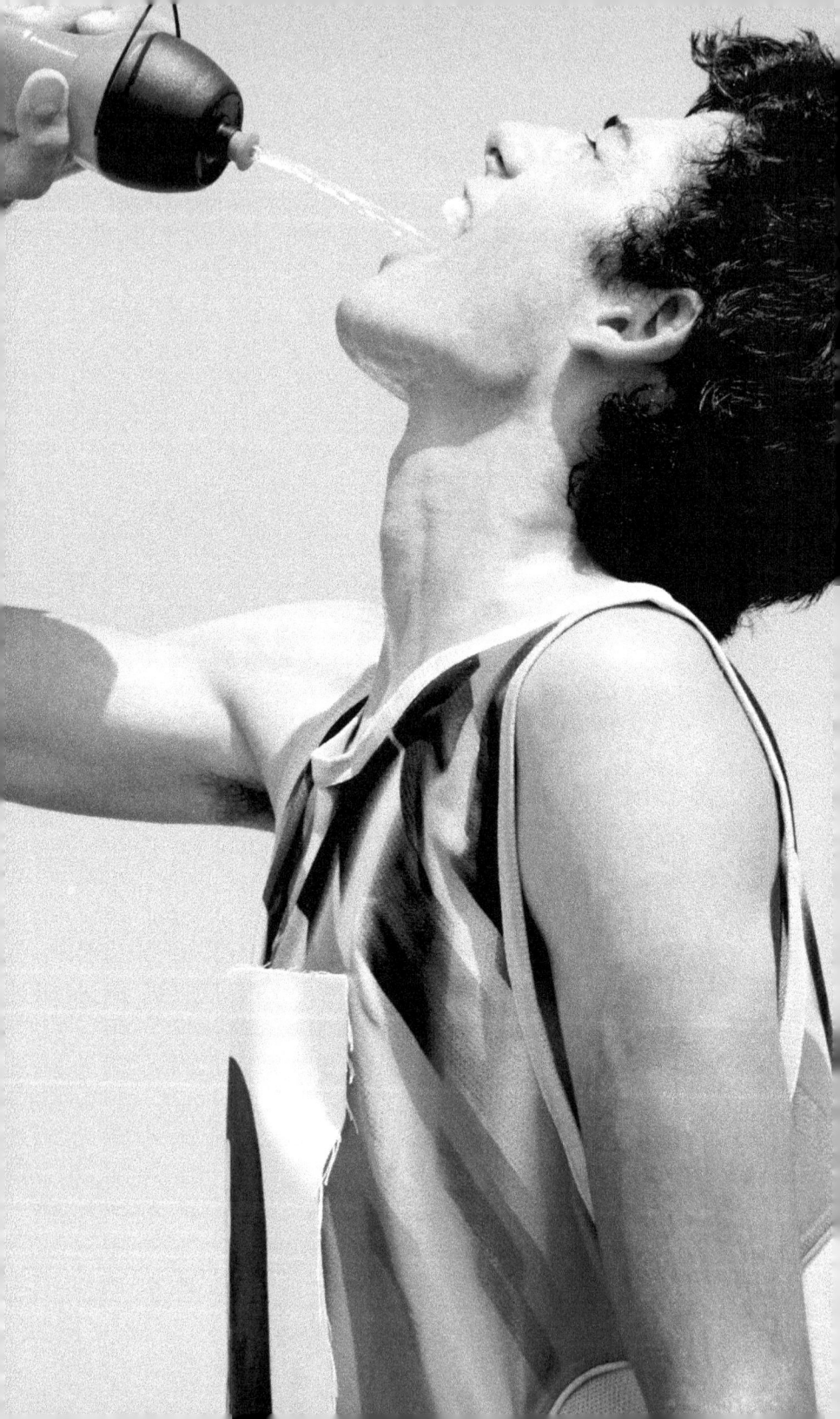

6. HYDRATE:

MAKE SURE YOU STAY HYDRATED, IT IS REALLY IMPORTANT FOR PERFORMING AT YOUR BEST. DRINK ENOUGH WATER ALL DAY, ESPECIALLY WHEN YOU ARE WORKING OUT. IT IS RECOMMENDED TO DRINK 8 CUPS OF WATER PER DAY. IF YOU ARE WORKING OUT IT IS RECOMMENDED TO DRINK AN EXTRA 8 OUNCES OF WATER FOR EVERY 20 MINUTES OF EXERCISE. EACH PERSON'S NEEDS ARE DIFFERENT SO IT IS IMPORTANT TO PAY ATTENTION TO YOUR BODY'S NEEDS AND HYDRATE ACCORDINGLY.

DRINKING WATER IS IDEAL FOR EVERYDAY HYDRATION AND SHORT DURATION ACTIVITIES. SPORTS DRINKS ARE EFFECTIVE DURING INTENSE EXERCISE LASTING OVER AN HOUR; THEY CONTAIN ELECTROLYTES LIKE SODIUM AND POTASSIUM TO REPLENISH THOSE LOST IN SWEAT. HOWEVER, SPORTS DRINKS ARE HIGH IN SUGAR, SO BE CAUTIOUS ABOUT DRINKING THEM TOO OFTEN.

7. ADAPTABILITY:

STAY OPEN TO FEEDBACK AND BE READY TO CHANGE UP HOW YOU TRAIN, HOW YOU PLAY, OR HOW YOU APPROACH THE GAME. BEING FLEXIBLE AND LEARNING FROM BOTH THE GOOD AND NOT-SO-GOOD MOMENTS HELPS YOU KEEP GETTING BETTER.

IF YOU ARE NOT THE MOST ATHLETIC AND DO NOT HAVE THE NATURAL ABILITIES THAT SOME OF YOUR PEERS HAVE, FOCUS ON YOUR FUNDAMENTALS. EMPHASIZE MASTERING THE BASICS OF YOUR SPORT LIKE TECHNIQUE, STRATEGY, AND UNDERSTANDING THE GAME. DEVELOPING A STRONG FOUNDATION IN THESE AREAS CAN COMPENSATE FOR ATHLETIC ADVANTAGES OTHERS MAY HAVE, ALLOWING YOU TO EXCEL THROUGH DISCIPLINE AND SKILL. REMEMBER, CONSISTENCY AND DEDICATION TO MASTERING FUNDAMENTALS OFTEN LEAD TO LONG TERM SUCCESS. STAY COMMITTED TO HOW OFTEN YOU TRAIN, STAY POSITIVE, AND ENJOY THE PROCESS OF BECOMING A BETTER PLAYER.

"IN THE END, IT'S EXTRA EFFORT THAT SEPARATES A WINNER FROM SECOND PLACE. BUT WINNING TAKES A LOT MORE THAT, TOO. IT STARTS WITH COMPLETE COMMAND OF THE FUNDAMENTALS. THEN IT TAKES DESIRE, DETERMINATION, DISCIPLINE, AND SELF-SACRIFICE. AND FINALLY, IT TAKES A GREAT DEAL OF LOVE, FAIRNESS AND RESPECT FOR YOUR FELLOW MAN. PUT ALL THESE TOGETHER, AND EVEN IF YOU DON'T WIN, HOW CAN YOU LOSE?"

- JESSE OWENS,
FOUR-TIME OLYMPIC GOLD MEDALIST

Food Group	Benefits
Meats	High Protein: Essential for muscle growth and repair. Rich in Iron: Prevents anemia and boosts energy. Vitamin B12: Supports nerve function and blood cell production. Zinc: Boosts the immune system and aids in metabolism.
Vegetables	Vitamins and Minerals: Provides essential nutrients like Vitamin A, C, K, and folate. Fiber: Aids digestion and promotes a healthy gut. Antioxidants: Protects against cell damage and reduces risk of chronic diseases. Low in Calories: Helps maintain a healthy weight.
Fruits	Vitamins and Minerals: High in Vitamin C, potassium, and folate. Fiber: Supports digestive health and regulates blood sugar. Antioxidants: Reduces inflammation and lowers the risk of chronic diseases. Natural Sugars: Provides a healthy energy boost.
Legumes	High Protein: Great plant-based protein source. Fiber: Improves digestion and heart health. Iron and Folate: Supports blood health and cell growth. Low Glycemic Index: Helps manage blood sugar levels.
Grains	Complex Carbohydrates: Provides sustained energy. Fiber: Promotes digestive health and prevents constipation. B Vitamins: Supports metabolism and energy production. Minerals: Provides iron, magnesium, and selenium for various bodily functions.

THE PERFECT FIT

NICE COACHES VS. STRICT COACHES, WHICH IS RIGHT FOR YOU? CHOOSING BETWEEN NICE AND STRICT COACHES DEPENDS ON YOUR PERSONALITY AND PREFERENCES. FINDING A BALANCE BETWEEN FIRMNESS AND ENCOURAGEMENT IS CRUCIAL FOR EFFECTIVE COACHING AND YOUR DEVELOPMENT. IT IS IMPORTANT TO PICK THE RIGHT COACHING STYLE FOR YOU.

IT IS ASSUMED THAT KIDS OFTEN BENEFIT MORE FROM NICE COACHES THAN STRICT COACHES. NICE COACHES CREATE A POSITIVE AND SUPPORTIVE ENVIRONMENT, CREATING CONFIDENCE AND A LOVE FOR THE SPORT. A NICE COACH MAY EASE STRESS AND ALLOW YOU TO BE MORE CREATIVE WITH YOUR GAME.

WHEN ATHLETES FEEL UNDERSTOOD AND SUPPORTED BY THEIR COACH, THEY ARE MORE LIKELY TO PUSH THEMSELVES, TAKE RISKS, AND ULTIMATELY PERFORM BETTER. A COACH'S ABILITY TO ADAPT THEIR STYLE TO SUIT INDIVIDUAL ATHLETES CAN ALSO PROMOTE RESILIENCE, HELPING THEM NAVIGATE CHALLENGES AND SETBACKS MORE EFFECTIVELY. ON THE OTHER HAND, STRICT COACHES MAY DISCOURAGE KIDS, LEADING TO LOWER SELF-ESTEEM AND MAKE PLAYING THE SPORT LESS ENJOYABLE. A STRICT COACH MIGHT LIMIT YOUR PERFORMANCE BY MAKING YOU AFRAID OF MAKING MISTAKES. POSITIVE REINFORCEMENT TENDS TO YIELD BETTER LONG-TERM RESULTS IN SKILL DEVELOPMENT AND OVERALL WELL-BEING.

WHILE IT IS GENERALLY PREFERRED TO HAVE SUPPORTIVE AND POSITIVE COACHES, SOME THINK THAT KIDS MAY BENEFIT FROM STRICT COACHES IN CERTAIN SITUATIONS. STRICT COACHES MIGHT INSTILL DISCIPLINE, RESILIENCE, AND A DRIVE TO PROVE THEMSELVES. HOWEVER, THIS APPROACH CAN ALSO LEAD TO STRESS, ANXIETY, AND DECREASED ENJOYMENT.

MY COLLEGE COACH WAS VERY STRICT; SOME PLAYERS MADE IT, OTHERS DIDN'T. I REMEMBER ONE DAY AT BASKETBALL PRACTICE, MY COACH THREW A BALL AT A TEAMMATE AND SHE QUIT THE TEAM.

THIS WAS LIKELY THE BEST DECISION FOR HER, AS SHE REALIZED SHE NEEDED A DIFFERENT COACHING STYLE. THE ONES WHO STAYED THRIVED UNDER HIS COACHING STYLE. IT MADE US A TEAM WHO COMPETED IN PRACTICE, WE PUSHED EACH OTHER TO BE BETTER PLAYERS, WE ALL HAD A WINNING MENTALITY, WHICH RESULTED IN US WINNING CHAMPIONSHIPS.

FINDING THE RIGHT COACHING STYLE IS NOT JUST ABOUT FINDING A NICE OR STRICT COACH. IT IS ALSO IMPORTANT TO FIND A COACH THAT ALIGNS WITH YOUR LEARNING PREFERENCES WHICH WILL IMPROVE COMMUNICATION AND YOUR UNDERSTANDING, MAKING IT EASIER FOR YOU TO ABSORB AND IMPLEMENT. THE RIGHT COACHING STYLE CREATES A POSITIVE ENVIRONMENT THAT BOOSTS YOUR MOTIVATION AND CONFIDENCE. A COMPATIBLE COACHING STYLE WILL HELP BUILD A STRONG RELATIONSHIP BETWEEN YOU AND YOUR COACH, WHICH IS IMPORTANT FOR TRUST AND OPEN COMMUNICATION. THIS RELATIONSHIP CAN LEAD TO GREATER ACCOUNTABILITY AND COMMITMENT FROM YOU, AS YOU WILL FEEL MORE CONNECTED AND INVESTED IN YOUR TRAINING AND PERFORMANCE. FINDING THE RIGHT COACHING STYLE CAN SIGNIFICANTLY IMPACT YOUR EXPERIENCE, GROWTH, AND ACHIEVEMENTS IN YOUR SPORT, SO CHOOSE WISELY.

THE RIGHT COACH FOR YOU DEPENDS ON YOUR PERSONALITY, PREFERENCES, AND GOALS. IF YOU THRIVE IN A POSITIVE AND SUPPORTIVE ENVIRONMENT, A NICE COACH MAY BE THE BETTER FIT, PROMOTING ENJOYMENT AND SKILL DEVELOPMENT. ON THE OTHER HAND, IF YOU RESPOND WELL TO TOUGH LOVE, A STRICT COACH MIGHT PUSH YOU TO OVERCOME CHALLENGES AND BUILD RESILIENCE. THINK ABOUT YOUR OWN NEEDS AND COMMUNICATION STYLE TO DETERMINE WHICH COACHING APPROACH IS BEST FOR YOU.

"A GOOD COACH CAN CHANGE A GAME. A GREAT COACH CAN CHANGE A LIFE."

-JOHN WOODEN,
LEGENDARY BASKETBALL COACH

PRACTICE HOW YOU PLAY

PUTTING IN THE WORK DURING PRACTICE REALLY IMPACTS HOW WELL YOU PLAY IN THE GAME. IF YOU PRACTICE YOUR MOVES AT FULL SPEED, YOU WILL BE READY TO NAIL THEM WHEN IT REALLY COUNTS. IF YOU PRACTICE AT HALF SPEED, YOU WILL NOT BE READY FOR A FAST-PACED GAME BECAUSE YOU HAVE ONLY MASTERED THE MOVE AT A SLOWER PACE. REMEMBER, THE SPEED AT WHICH YOU PLAY IS DIFFERENT FROM OTHERS, SO FOCUS ON PRACTICING AT YOUR GAME PACE, WHERE YOU FEEL COMFORTABLE AND IN CONTROL. SENECA, A ROMAN STOIC PHILOSOPHER SAID, *"LUCK IS WHERE PREPARATION MEETS OPPORTUNITY."* YOU DON'T WANT TO BE THAT PERSON WHO HAS THE OPPORTUNITY BUT YOU ARE NOT PREPARED. DURING PRACTICE,

ALWAYS GIVE YOUR BEST EFFORT ON BOTH OFFENSE AND DEFENSE, SO YOU ARE READY AND YOU DO NOT FEEL RUSHED DURING THE ACTUAL GAME. ENCOURAGE YOUR TEAMMATES TO PLAY THEIR BEST DEFENSE AGAINST YOU. THIS WILL HELP YOU BE BETTER PREPARED FOR GAMES. IF YOUR TEAMMATES ARE SLACKING ON DEFENSE AGAINST YOU, WHAT DO YOU THINK WILL HAPPEN DURING A GAME WHEN YOU ARE UP AGAINST A GREAT DEFENDER OR ONE WHO IS GIVING THEIR ALL? YOU MIGHT NOT PERFORM AS WELL BECAUSE YOU HAVE NOT PREPARED AGAINST THIS TYPE OF DEFENSE. RUN YOUR SPRINTS AT FULL SPEED SO YOU WON'T BE EASILY TIRED DURING THE GAME. THE MORE TIRED YOU ARE, THE MORE EFFORT IT TAKES TO CONCENTRATE, AND THE MORE LIKELY YOU ARE TO MAKE MISTAKES. PREPARE HARD DURING PRACTICE SO THAT THE GAME COMES EASY. SO REMEMBER, SLACKING AT PRACTICE DOES NOT HELP YOU OR YOUR TEAMMATES. PRACTICE GAME SITUATIONS, BEING COMMITTED AND DEDICATED IS KEY TO SUCCEEDING.

IN PRACTICE, YOU HAVE TO PUSH YOURSELF TO THE POINT OF EXHAUSTION. WHEN YOU ARE RUNNING SUICIDES OR SEVENTEENS YOU ARE SUPPOSED TO BE TIRED; THAT'S HOW YOU GET BETTER. A SIMPLE WAY TO FIGHT THROUGH YOUR EXHAUSTION AND SHOW MENTAL TOUGHNESS IS TO TAKE YOUR MIND SOMEPLACE ELSE. THINK OF A PLACE YOU WOULD LOVE TO BE OR SOMETHING YOU LOVE TO DO,

AND ENVISION YOURSELF THERE, DOING WHAT YOU LOVE. TAKING YOUR MIND OFF HOW TIRED YOU ARE WILL HELP YOU PUSH THROUGH YOUR STRUGGLES.

BY PRACTICING AND TRAINING IN SITUATIONS THAT EMULATE ACTUAL GAMEPLAY, YOU WILL DEVELOP YOUR SKILLS AND DECISION-MAKING UNDER REALISTIC CONDITIONS. BY REPLICATING GAMEPLAY DURING PRACTICE, YOU CAN SLOW THE GAME DOWN MENTALLY, WHICH WILL HELP YOUR ABILITY TO PROCESS INFORMATION, REACT TO DIFFERENT SCENARIOS, AND PLAY WITH CONFIDENCE. THIS TYPE OF PRACTICE HELPS YOU TO THINK CRITICALLY ABOUT YOUR CHOICES, WHETHER IT'S DECIDING WHEN TO PASS, SHOOT, OR DEFEND. BY REPEATEDLY FACING THESE SITUATIONS IN PRACTICE, YOU CAN BREAK DOWN PLAYS INTO SMALLER PARTS, HELPING YOU LEARN THE GAME AND DEVELOP A BETTER UNDERSTANDING OF THE GAME'S FLOW.

TRAINING IN GAME-LIKE CONDITIONS ALLOWS COACHES TO PROVIDE IMMEDIATE FEEDBACK, HELPING YOU TO GET BETTER. BY FOCUSING ON SPECIFIC ASPECTS OF YOUR GAME DURING PRACTICE, YOU CAN IDENTIFY AREAS FOR IMPROVEMENT AND WORK ON THEM IN REAL TIME, ENSURING THAT YOU ARE READY FOR THE ACTUAL GAME.

EFFORT AND ATTITUDE

THERE ARE TWO THINGS YOU CAN CONTROL; EFFORT AND ATTITUDE. EFFORT IS THE ENERGY AND HARD WORK YOU PUT INTO SOMETHING. IT'S THE DETERMINATION AND DEDICATION YOU SHOW WHEN TRYING TO REACH YOUR GOALS OR IMPROVE YOUR SKILLS. EFFORT INVOLVES DOING THE WORK, KEEP GOING THROUGH CHALLENGES, AND CONSISTENTLY WORKING TOWARD GETTING BETTER. IT'S THE DIFFERENCE BETWEEN WAKING UP AT 5:00AM TO GO TO THE GYM BEFORE SCHOOL OR WORK OR DECIDING TO SLEEP IN.

TO GIVE GREAT EFFORT IN SPORTS, FOCUS ON CONSISTENT AND INTENSE PRACTICE TO IMPROVE YOUR SKILLS. DURING GAMES, STAY COMMITTED TO EVERY PLAY, HUSTLE ON BOTH OFFENSE AND

DEFENSE, AND PUSH YOURSELF BEYOND YOUR COMFORT ZONE. MAINTAIN A POSITIVE ATTITUDE, LEARN FROM MISTAKES, AND APPROACH CHALLENGES WITH DETERMINATION. PUTTING IN EXTRA WORK DURING TRAINING AND CONSISTENTLY GIVING YOUR ALL DURING COMPETITIONS WILL CONTRIBUTE TO DELIVERING GREAT EFFORT.

EFFORT IS THE DRIVING FORCE BEHIND GETTING BETTER AND WINNING. IT HELPS YOU DEVELOP SKILLS, OVERCOME CHALLENGES, AND PERFORM AT YOUR BEST. WITHOUT EFFORT, PROGRESS BECOMES LIMITED, AND ACHIEVING YOUR GOALS BECOMES MORE CHALLENGING. EFFORT IS LIKE THE STARTING POINT FOR GROWING PERSONALLY, ALLOWING YOU TO PUSH BOUNDARIES AND REACH YOUR FULL POTENTIAL.

IMAGINE HUSTLING DOWN THE ENTIRE BASKETBALL COURT TO STOP AN OPPONENT FROM SCORING EASILY. THAT IS NOT JUST PLAYING DEFENSE; IT IS GIVING YOUR ALL, SHOWING YOU ARE COMMITTED TO THE TEAM, AND WILLING TO GO THAT EXTRA MILE. PICTURE THIS: YOU ARE PUTTING IN A BURST OF ENERGY IN THE LAST MINUTES OF A SOCCER GAME, ZIPPING PAST DEFENDERS, AND SCORING A GAME CHANGING GOAL. IT IS NOT JUST ABOUT SKILL; IT IS ABOUT PUTTING IN EXCEPTIONAL EFFORT, PROVING YOUR DETERMINATION, ESPECIALLY WHEN THE

PRESSURE IS ON. THINK ABOUT RUNNING A MARATHON, IT IS NOT JUST ABOUT PHYSICAL STRENGTH BUT ALSO MENTAL TOUGHNESS. PUSHING THROUGH TIREDNESS, KEEPING A STEADY PACE, AND CROSSING THAT FINISH LINE TAKES AN EXTRAORDINARY AMOUNT OF EFFORT, BOTH PHYSICALLY AND MENTALLY. ALL THESE EXAMPLES HIGHLIGHT GREAT EFFORT IN SPORTS. I CAN REMEMBER BEING DOWN BY 26 POINTS IN A BASKETBALL GAME WITH EIGHT MINUTES TO GO AND COMING BACK TO WIN BY THREE POINTS. WE COULD HAVE GOTTEN FRUSTRATED, PUT OUR HEADS DOWN, AND FELL APART AS A TEAM, BUT INSTEAD, WE STAYED FOCUSED, HELD OUR HEADS HIGH, AND PUSHED HARDER. WITHOUT THAT EFFORT, THIS WIN WOULD HAVE BEEN IMPOSSIBLE.

TO IMPROVE YOUR EFFORT START WITH DEVELOPING A GROWTH MINDSET AS DISCUSSED IN THIS BOOK. SET CLEAR GOALS AND COMMIT TO A CONSISTENT PRACTICE ROUTINE. BE OPEN TO FEEDBACK, EVEN WHEN IT'S TOUGH, AND USE IT AS A TOOL TO IMPROVE. STAY MENTALLY PRESENT AND ENGAGED DURING PRACTICE, RATHER THAN JUST GOING THROUGH THE MOTIONS. HAVE YOU EVER FELT LIKE YOU WERE ABOUT TO THROW UP AFTER A HARD PRACTICE OF CONDITIONING? THAT'S WHEN YOU KNOW YOU HAVE GIVEN YOUR ALL. BUILD A STRONG ROUTINE FOR PREPARATION AND CONDITIONING, SO YOU HAVE THE PHYSICAL

AND MENTAL STAMINA NEEDED TO PUSH THROUGH WHEN THINGS GET TOUGH. PRACTICING VISUALIZATION CAN ALSO BE HELPFUL; SEE YOURSELF GIVING YOUR BEST EFFORT IN GAMES AND TRAINING SESSIONS, AND FEEL THE MOTIVATION THAT BRINGS. AFTER EACH PRACTICE OR GAME TAKE THE TIME TO THINK ABOUT WHERE YOUR EFFORT WAS STRONGEST AND WHERE YOU COULD PUSH HARDER. BY BEING INTENTIONAL ABOUT YOUR EFFORT, YOU CAN STRENGTHEN YOUR COMMITMENT, RESILIENCE, AND PERFORMANCE.

ATTITUDE IS YOUR OUTLOOK, FEELINGS, AND BEHAVIORS TOWARDS SOMETHING OR SOMEONE. IT IS HOW YOU TACKLE THE GAME, PRACTICE, OR WORKOUTS. IT INVOLVES YOUR MINDSET, BELIEFS AND APPROACH, WHICH INFLUENCES HOW YOU RESPOND IN A SITUATION OR HOW YOU INTERACT WITH COACHES, TEAMMATES OR REFEREES. BEING POSITIVE CAN MAKE TOUGH TASKS SEEM LESS SCARY, BUT A NEGATIVE ATTITUDE MIGHT MESS WITH HOW WELL YOU PLAY. YOUR ATTITUDE IS BASICALLY THE MINDSET YOU CARRY INTO THE GAME OR SPORT.

A PLAYER WITH A BAD ATTITUDE WILL DISPLAY POOR SPORTSMANSHIP BY ARGUING WITH TEAMMATES, OPPONENTS, OR REFEREES. THEY MAY BLAME OTHERS FOR MISTAKES OR SHOW A LACK OF RESPECT TO THE COACH.

A PLAYER WITH A BAD ATTITUDE CAN SIGNIFICANTLY IMPACT THE TEAM'S CHEMISTRY. NEGATIVE ENERGY FROM ONE PLAYER OFTEN CREATES A RIPPLE EFFECT THAT CAN SPREAD TO OTHERS, LEADING TO FRUSTRATION, RESENTMENT, AND DISTRACTIONS FROM TEAM GOALS. WHEN A PLAYER IS ALWAYS NEGATIVE, WHETHER THROUGH COMPLAINING, LACK OF EFFORT, OR DISRESPECT TOWARD TEAMMATES AND COACHES, IT CAN LOWER THE TEAM'S MOTIVATION AND BRING DOWN THE TEAM SPIRIT. OTHERS MIGHT START TO COPY THIS ATTITUDE, ESPECIALLY YOUNGER OR MORE IMPRESSIONABLE PLAYERS, CREATING A TOXIC ENVIRONMENT THAT'S HARD TO REVERSE. DON'T BE THAT PLAYER WITH A BAD ATTITUDE. IN TEAM SPORTS, UNITY AND TRUST ARE KEY. A PLAYER WITH A BAD ATTITUDE NOT ONLY DISRUPTS TEAM COMMUNICATION AND COOPERATION ON THE FIELD OR COURT BUT ALSO DAMAGES RELATIONSHIPS OFF IT. THE TEAM'S FOCUS CAN SHIFT FROM ACHIEVING GOALS TO MANAGING OR AVOIDING CONFLICT, ULTIMATELY HARMING THEIR CHANCES OF SUCCESS. FOR A TEAM TO REACH ITS FULL POTENTIAL, EVERY MEMBER MUST BE INVESTED IN THE SAME VISION, LIFT EACH OTHER UP, AND MAINTAIN A POSITIVE, SUPPORTIVE ATMOSPHERE. TEAMS THAT ADDRESS ATTITUDE ISSUES EARLY MAKE IT CLEAR THAT IT WILL NOT BE TOLERATED. BE THE PLAYER THAT CREATES THE TEAM'S WINNING MENTALITY THAT BENEFITS EVERYONE.

A BAD ATTITUDE CAN BE A MAJOR RED FLAG FOR COACHES AND RECRUITERS, WHICH CAN PREVENT YOU FROM BEING RECRUITED. WHEN SCOUTS AND COACHES ARE EVALUATING PLAYERS, THEY'RE NOT ONLY LOOKING AT PHYSICAL SKILLS AND PERFORMANCE, THEY'RE ALSO LOOKING AT ATTITUDE, EFFORT, AND HOW WELL YOU FIT INTO A TEAM ENVIRONMENT. A PLAYER WITH A POOR ATTITUDE, WHO DOESN'T SHOW RESPECT FOR COACHES, TEAMMATES, OR THE GAME ITSELF, RISKS BEING SEEN AS A POTENTIAL DISRUPTION TO TEAM CHEMISTRY. COACHES VALUE PLAYERS WHO BRING POSITIVE ENERGY, ARE COACHABLE, AND RESILIENT. A BAD ATTITUDE WILL RUIN YOUR CHANCES OF GETTING RECRUITED MORE THAN HAVING A BAD GAME, SO CHECK YOUR ATTITUDE BEFORE WALKING IN THE GYM.

A PLAYER WITH A GREAT ATTITUDE WILL ENCOURAGE THEIR TEAMMATES DURING FAVORABLE AND CHALLENGING MOMENTS. THEY WILL SHOW RESPECT TOWARDS OPPONENTS, COACHES, AND REFEREES. HAVING A POSITIVE ATTITUDE IS GREAT FOR TEAM SPORTS BECAUSE IT BOOSTS MORALE, STRENGTHENS TEAMWORK, AND HELPS BUILD TRUST AMONG TEAMMATES. A POSITIVE MINDSET ENCOURAGES PLAYERS TO SUPPORT ONE ANOTHER, STAY FOCUSED ON SHARED GOALS, AND HANDLE CHALLENGES WITH RESILIENCE. WHEN EVERYONE BRINGS A POSITIVE ATTITUDE,

IT CREATES AN UPLIFTING ENVIRONMENT WHERE PLAYERS FEEL MOTIVATED TO PERFORM THEIR BEST AND WORK TOGETHER, LEADING TO A STRONGER, MORE COHESIVE TEAM. YOUR POSITIVE ATTITUDE CAN HAVE A POWERFUL INFLUENCE ON YOUR TEAM BY SETTING A TONE OF ENCOURAGEMENT AND RESILIENCE THAT OTHERS WANT TO FOLLOW. WHEN YOU BRING ENERGY, OPTIMISM, AND A WILLINGNESS TO KEEP PUSHING EVEN WHEN THINGS GET TOUGH, YOU INSPIRE THOSE AROUND YOU TO ADOPT THE SAME MINDSET. TEAMMATES ARE MORE LIKELY TO STAY MOTIVATED, GIVE THEIR BEST EFFORT, AND BOUNCE BACK FROM MISTAKES WHEN THEY SEE SOMEONE LEADING WITH POSITIVITY. A POSITIVE ATTITUDE CREATES A SUPPORTIVE ENVIRONMENT WHERE PLAYERS FEEL VALUED AND UNITED, WHICH CAN IMPROVE TEAM CHEMISTRY AND TRUST. BY BEING A SOURCE OF POSITIVITY, YOU HELP YOUR TEAM STAY FOCUSED ON GOALS, STAY CONFIDENT UNDER PRESSURE, AND BUILD A CULTURE OF RESILIENCE AND MUTUAL SUPPORT. MAINTAINING A POSITIVE ATTITUDE INVOLVES ACCEPTING RESPONSIBILITY FOR YOUR MISTAKES, AND KEEPING A DETERMINED AND FOCUSED MINDSET FOR THE ENTIRE GAME.

YOUR BODY LANGUAGE IS CONNECTED TO YOUR ATTITUDE TOO. YOUR BODY LANGUAGE INTRODUCES YOU BEFORE YOU SPEAK. IT "SPILLS THE BEANS" ABOUT HOW YOU ARE FEELING.

POOR BODY LANGUAGE WILL ALSO INDICATE A BAD ATTITUDE. IF YOU DROP YOUR HEAD, IT LOOKS LIKE YOU ARE NOT FEELING GREAT ABOUT HOW YOU ARE PLAYING. IF YOU THROW YOUR HANDS UP OR GRAB YOUR HEAD, IT SHOWS YOU ARE FRUSTRATED. PUTTING YOUR HANDS ON YOUR HIPS OR SLOUCHING CAN BE A SIGN THAT YOU ARE TIRED. COACHES REACT TO YOUR BODY LANGUAGE. IF YOU LOOK FRUSTRATED OR TIRED, THE COACH MAY PULL YOU OUT THE GAME. KEEPING YOUR BODY LANGUAGE POSITIVE IS CRUCIAL BECAUSE IT NOT ONLY INFLUENCES HOW OTHERS SEE YOU BUT ALSO IMPACTS YOUR OWN MINDSET AND PERFORMANCE. POSITIVE BODY LANGUAGE CAN BOOST YOUR CONFIDENCE, COMMUNICATE A WINNING ATTITUDE TO TEAMMATES, AND EVEN TRICK YOUR BRAIN INTO FEELING MORE OPTIMISTIC. IT HELPS IMPROVE THE ATMOSPHERE, TEAMWORK, AND CONTRIBUTES TO A BETTER EXPERIENCE IN SPORTS.

I HAD A TEAMMATE THAT WOULD GET FRUSTRATED WHEN SHE MISSED A SHOT, AND THE WHOLE GYM NOTICED BECAUSE HER BODY LANGUAGE SHOWED IT. SHE WOULD HIT HER THIGH, ROLL HER EYES, MAYBE EVEN YELL OUT A CURSE WORD, THEN JOG BACK AND BARELY STAY FOCUSED ON DEFENSE. WHEN THE COACH WOULD TAKE HER OUT OF THE GAME, SHE WOULD EXPRESS THAT SHE WAS UPSET BECAUSE SHE MISSED A FEW SHOTS.

BUT IN REALITY, NO ONE ELSE WAS COUNTING HER MISSED SHOTS, SHE WAS THE ONLY ONE KEEPING TRACK. WHAT GOT HER PULLED FROM THE GAME WASN'T THE MISSED SHOTS; IT WAS HER BODY LANGUAGE. DEVELOPING A "NEXT-PLAY" MINDSET IS CRUCIAL FOR STAYING COMPOSED AND FOCUSED ON WHAT'S AHEAD, NOT WHAT'S ALREADY HAPPENED. IF YOU PLAN TO PLAY SPORTS IN COLLEGE, YOUR ATTITUDE, EFFORT AND BODY LANGUAGE MAY BE A COACH'S DECIDING FACTOR IN WHETHER THEY DECIDE TO RECRUIT YOU OR NOT. YOU CAN BE THE BEST PLAYER ON YOUR TEAM, BUT IF YOU HAVE A BAD ATTITUDE, LACK EFFORT, OR POOR BODY LANGUAGE, COLLEGE COACHES MAY PASS ON RECRUITING YOU. REMEMBER, BEING A COACHABLE PLAYER WILL SET YOU APART. BOOSTING YOUR ATTITUDE IN SPORTS IS ABOUT KNOWING YOURSELF AND TAKING SPECIFIC STEPS. I HAVE LISTED 6 STEPS BELOW THAT CAN HELP YOUR JOURNEY:

1. POSITIVE SELF-TALK

SWITCH OUT THOSE NEGATIVE THOUGHTS WITH POSITIVE VIBES. WHEN THINGS GET TOUGH, BE YOUR OWN CHEERLEADER AND FOCUS ON WHAT YOU ARE DOING WELL. TELL YOURSELF THINGS LIKE, "I CAN DO THIS," I TRUST MY SKILLS," "ON TO THE NEXT PLAY," "I AM READY FOR THIS," OR "I STAY CALM UNDER PRESSURE."

2. REALISTIC GOALS

SET GOALS THAT YOU CAN ACTUALLY REACH. CELEBRATE THE SMALL WINS; THEY ARE CONFIDENCE BOOSTERS THAT HELP YOU KEEP A POSITIVE MINDSET.

3. LEARN FROM MISTAKES

INSTEAD OF GETTING STUCK ON MISTAKES, SEE THEM AS CHANCES TO GET BETTER. FIGURE OUT WHAT WENT WRONG, ADJUST, AND KEEP MOVING FORWARD WITH A POSITIVE MINDSET AND A POSITIVE ATTITUDE.

4. CHEER ON TEAMMATES

BE A GOOD TEAMMATE: SUPPORT OTHERS AND CELEBRATE THEIR VICTORIES. A POSITIVE TEAM VIBE ADDS TO YOUR OWN POSITIVE ATTITUDE.

BEING A GOOD TEAMMATE INVOLVES MORE THAN JUST PLAYING WELL TOGETHER; IT IS ABOUT FOSTERING TRUST, SUPPORT, AND COLLABORATION WITHIN THE TEAM. YOU CAN BE A GOOD TEAMMATE BY COMMUNICATING EFFECTIVELY, LISTENING ACTIVELY, AND RESPECTING OTHERS' OPINIONS AND CONTRIBUTIONS. ALSO, SHOW EMPATHY AND ENCOURAGEMENT, LIFTING TEAM MORALE DURING BOTH WINS AND LOSSES. BE RELIABLE, SHOW UP PREPARED AND COMMITTED TO YOUR ROLE, WHILE ALSO BEING ADAPTABLE AND WILLING TO STEP UP WHEN NEEDED. PRIORITIZE THE TEAM'S GOALS ABOVE YOUR OWN PERSONAL RECOGNITION. CELEBRATE THE SUCCESSES OF OTHERS AND OFFER CONSTRUCTIVE FEEDBACK TO HELP THE TEAM IMPROVE AS A WHOLE. CREATE A POSITIVE AND INCLUSIVE TEAM ENVIRONMENT WHERE EVERY MEMBER FEELS VALUED AND MOTIVATED TO GIVE THEIR BEST EFFORT.

5. EMBRACE FEEDBACK

SEEK ADVICE AS A WAY TO GET BETTER, NOT AS CRITICISM. USE IT AS A TOOL TO GROW; IT'S ALL ABOUT BECOMING A STRONGER PLAYER AND PERSON. COACHES, PARENTS AND FRIENDS GIVE YOU ADVICE TO HELP YOU, NOT TO MAKE YOU FEEL BAD. LISTEN TO WHAT THEY HAVE TO SAY WITH A POSITIVE ATTITUDE AND TRY APPLYING IT TO YOUR GAMES, PRACTICES AND TRAINING. SOMETIMES YOU NEED ACCOUNTABILITY TO PUSH YOU TO BE YOUR BEST SELF. IT DOES NOT HURT TO LOOK IN THE MIRROR AND ACKNOWLEDGE THAT YOU COULD BE THE PROBLEM. EMBRACE THEIR GUIDANCE, WORK ON YOUR WEAKNESSES, AND STRIVE TO GROW BOTH ON AND OFF THE FIELD OR COURT.

PUTTING IN EFFORT AND KEEPING A POSITIVE ATTITUDE CAN TOTALLY CHANGE HOW YOU SEE THINGS. WHEN YOU WORK HARD, YOU FEEL ACCOMPLISHED AND TOUGH, WHICH MAKES YOUR MINDSET MORE POSITIVE. HAVING A GOOD ATTITUDE ALSO HELPS YOU LOOK AT CHALLENGES WITH OPTIMISM, MAKING IT EASIER TO BOUNCE BACK FROM TOUGH LOSSES OR SITUATIONS. MIXING EFFORT AND A POSITIVE ATTITUDE GIVES YOU A MINDSET THAT IS READY TO GROW, ADAPT, AND STAY OPEN TO NEW CHALLENGES. AND HEY, DEVELOPING A POSITIVE ATTITUDE TAKES TIME, SO BE COOL WITH YOURSELF AS YOU WORK ON IT.

6. STAY IN THE MOMENT

FOCUS ON WHAT IS HAPPENING RIGHT NOW, NOT PAST SLIP-UPS OR FUTURE WORRIES. STAYING PRESENT KEEPS YOUR MIND POSITIVE AND SHARP. FOCUSING ON PAST MISTAKES WILL ONLY HINDER YOUR FUTURE PERFORMANCE, ENSURING YOU WILL HAVE A BAD GAME. HAVE YOU EVER SEEN A PLAYER GO 0 FOR 5 IN THE FIRST QUARTER, THEN GO 5 FOR 5 IN THE SECOND QUARTER? YES, IT'S POSSIBLE TO GET OFF TO A BAD START, THEN FINISH THE GAME WITH A CAREER HIGH. IN ORDER TO ACCOMPLISH THIS, YOU HAVE TO KEEP A POSITIVE MINDSET AND NOT LET A FEW MISSED SHOTS OR DROPPED PASSES CAUSE YOU TO HANG YOUR HEAD OR STOP PERFORMING AT YOUR BEST. I REMEMBER WATCHING STEPH CURRY IN GAME 6 OF THE WESTERN CONFERENCE SEMIFINALS AGAINST THE HOUSTON ROCKETS. STEPH WENT SCORELESS IN THE FIRST HALF. HIS TEAM WAS DOWN BY 7 POINTS AT THE BEGINNING OF THE FOURTH QUARTER BUT ENDED UP WINNING THE GAME BY 5 POINTS, ADVANCING TO THE WESTERN CONFERENCE FINALS. STEPH FINISHED THAT GAME WITH 33 POINTS. PROVING THAT JUST BECAUSE YOU START OFF PLAYING POORLY DOESN'T MEAN YOU WILL FINISH POORLY.

"YOU MISS 100% OF THE SHOTS YOU DON'T TAKE."

-WAYNE GRETZKY,
LEGENDARY HOCKEY PLAYER

THE POWER OF BEING IN SHAPE

MOST ATHLETE'S FOCUS THEIR TRAINING ON SKILLS LIKE SHOOTING, PASSING, HITTING, KICKING OR CATCHING, BUT MANY DO NOT PAY ENOUGH ATTENTION TO THE LESS EXCITING PARTS, LIKE CONDITIONING. BEING IN SHAPE IS THE FOUNDATION OF ALMOST EVERY SPORT. IT WILL BOOST YOUR ENDURANCE, STRENGTH, SPEED, AND AGILITY; ALL THE THINGS THAT HELP YOU SUCCEED. WHEN YOU ARE IN GREAT SHAPE, YOU FEEL MORE CONFIDENT, FOCUSED, AND MAKE SMART DECISIONS EVEN WHEN YOU ARE UNDER PRESSURE. CONDITIONING ALSO HELPS PREVENT INJURIES BY MAKING YOUR MUSCLES, JOINTS, AND LIGAMENTS STRONGER. PLUS, BEING WELL-CONDITIONED ENSURES YOU ARE PHYSICALLY PREPARED TO HANDLE WHATEVER COMES YOUR WAY.

CONDITIONING IS NOT JUST ABOUT PHYSICAL STRENGTH, IT IS ALSO ABOUT MENTAL TOUGHNESS. TRAINING REGULARLY, EVEN WHEN IT IS TOUGH, WILL HELP YOU BUILD YOUR MINDSET TO HANDLE PRESSURE AND KEEP GOING THROUGH CHALLENGES. FOR EXAMPLE, IF YOU'VE BEEN WORKING HARD AT CONDITIONING, YOU ARE MORE LIKELY TO FEEL CONFIDENT, STAY CALM, AND HANDLE SETBACKS WHEN THEY HAPPEN DURING A GAME. THIS KIND OF RESILIENCE FROM CONDITIONING WILL GIVE YOU A MENTAL EDGE WHEN IT COUNTS.

CONDITIONING CAN ALSO HELP YOU ADAPT TO YOUR COACH'S STYLE, ESPECIALLY IF IT'S FAST-PACED OR HIGH-INTENSITY. FOR A TEAM TO PLAY A QUICK, AGGRESSIVE GAME, EACH PLAYER NEEDS TO BE IN TOP SHAPE TO KEEP UP THE PACE WITHOUT LOSING FOCUS. WITHOUT PROPER CONDITIONING, PLAYERS TIRE FASTER, WHICH LEADS TO MISTAKES AND SLOWER REACTIONS. COACHES WHO RELY ON A FAST OFFENSE OR CONSTANT DEFENSE NEED THEIR ATHLETES TO BE WELL-CONDITIONED TO KEEP THE ENERGY UP AND WEAR DOWN THE OPPONENT.

MY COLLEGE COACH RAN A FAST-PACED GAME. HE PUSHED US TO PLAY PRESSURE DEFENSE FROM START TO FINISH, WITH A FULL-COURT PRESS THAT WE BECAME GREAT AT. OUR DEFENSE CREATED OUR OFFENSE. IT WAS A PUSH THE BALL UP THE

FLOOR, SCORE AND PRESS TYPE OF PLAY. FOR THIS REASON, THE COACH KNEW HE NEEDED PLAYERS THAT WERE IN EXCEPTIONAL SHAPE BEFORE THE SEASON STARTED. ONCE THE SEASON STARTED, THERE WAS NO TIME TO GET IN SHAPE. WE HAD TO FOCUS ON PLAYS, TEAM CHEMISTRY, DEFENSIVE SETS, THE PRESS, AND PRESS BREAK. IF YOU WERE NOT IN SHAPE BY THEN, YOU WERE ALREADY BEHIND. AS SOON AS WE STEPPED ON CAMPUS IN AUGUST, CONDITIONING FOR BASKETBALL SEASON STARTED. MY FIRST YEAR, THE DAY AFTER I MOVED INTO THE DORM, I WAS WALKING PAST THE TRACK AND SAW MY TEAMMATES RUNNING. THEY CALLED ME OVER, HOLDING ME ACCOUNTABLE. I DIDN'T KNOW CONDITIONING STARTED THAT SOON, BUT THE TEAM MADE SURE I KNEW THE EXPECTATIONS. WE RAN FIVE, SOMETIMES SIX, DAYS A WEEK WITH NO SLACKING, AND WE COMPETED IN EVERYTHING. THAT WORK MADE US THE BEST TEAM IN THE CENTRAL INTERCOLLEGIATE ATHLETIC ASSOCIATION (CIAA).

BE IN SHAPE BEFORE YOUR TRYOUTS. IF YOU ARE NOT, YOU WILL ALREADY BE BEHIND. TRYOUTS ARE NOT THE PLACE TO BE OUT OF SHAPE OR GASPING FOR AIR. IT IS YOUR TIME TO BE AT YOUR BEST, SHOWCASING EVERYTHING YOU HAVE BEEN TRAINING AND WORKING SO HARD FOR. SO, GET OUT THERE AND SHOW THEM WHAT YOU'VE GOT!

TO GET IN SHAPE, YOU NEED A BALANCED TRAINING PLAN THAT INCLUDES CARDIO, STRENGTH TRAINING, FLEXIBILITY, AND RECOVERY. CARDIO EXERCISES LIKE RUNNING OR CYCLING BUILD ENDURANCE, WHILE STRENGTH TRAINING WITH WEIGHTS OR BODYWEIGHT EXERCISES BUILDS POWER AND STABILITY. FLEXIBILITY EXERCISES LIKE STRETCHING OR YOGA IMPROVE RANGE OF MOTION AND REDUCE THE CHANCE OF INJURY. DO NOT FORGET TO REST, IT IS ESSENTIAL TO LET YOUR MUSCLES RECOVER AND GROW STRONGER. EATING HEALTHY ALSO HELPS, AS GOOD NUTRITION FUELS WORKOUTS AND SUPPORTS RECOVERY. MAKE SURE YOU ARE IN TIP TOP SHAPE BEFORE YOUR SEASON STARTS; IT WILL GIVE YOU A JUMP START ON THE COMPETITION.

PHOTO BY: DON ROCKY

FIND THAT DOG
IN YOU

THE DRIVE HAS TO COME FROM YOU, NOT YOUR PARENTS, COACHES, TRAINERS, OR ANY OTHER OUTSIDE PERSON. NOBODY CAN WANT YOUR SUCCESS MORE THAN YOU DO. YOU HAVE TO WANT TO PUSH YOURSELF BEYOND YOUR LIMITS, YOU HAVE TO WANT TO BE FEARLESS DURING THE GAME, AND YOU HAVE TO BELIEVE YOU ARE THE BEST. LET ME TELL YOU THIS: YOU ARE NOT WRONG TO BELIEVE YOU ARE THE BEST. YOU MUST APPROACH THE GAME WITH THE MINDSET THAT YOU WILL DO EVERYTHING TO WIN, NOT TO LOSE. MANY PLAYERS TAKE THEIR SHOTS THINKING, "I DON'T WANT TO MISS," OR PLAY WITH THE MINDSET OF, "I DON'T WANT TO MESS UP." PLAYING THAT WAY WILL GET YOU PUT ON THE BENCH. IF YOU SHOOT THE BALL TO NOT MISS, YOU WILL MORE THAN LIKELY MISS. SIMILARLY, IF YOU PLAY TO NOT MAKE MISTAKES, YOU WILL END UP MAKING MISTAKES. COACHES LOOK FOR PLAYERS WHO ARE CONFIDENT ENOUGH TO FAIL AND

PAY CLOSE ATTENTION TO HOW THEY BOUNCE BACK. "FIND THAT DOG IN YOU" AND PLAY TO MAKE A DIFFERENCE IN THE GAME. PLAYING WITH INTENSITY CAN CREATE OPPORTUNITIES FOR SUCCESS, WHETHER IT'S WINNING GAMES, EARNING AWARDS, OR ATTRACTING THE ATTENTION OF COACHES. WHEN YOU PLAY HARD, YOU PUSH YOUR PHYSICAL LIMITS, IMPROVE YOUR SKILLS, AND ENHANCE YOUR OVERALL GAME. THIS CAN INSPIRE YOUR TEAMMATES AND CREATE A STRONG TEAM CULTURE. HARD WORK MAKES A GAME CHANGER. BECOME A GAME CHANGER BY BRINGING OUT "THAT DOG IN YOU!"

TO PLAY WITH MORE INTENSITY, START BY SETTING CLEAR AND ACHIEVABLE GOALS FOR EACH GAME OR PRACTICE, PROVIDING YOU WITH FOCUS AND MOTIVATION. FOR EXAMPLE, IF YOU ARE A BASKETBALL PLAYER, YOU MIGHT SET A GAME GOAL TO SCORE 10 POINTS, GET ONE STEAL, AND ATTEMPT 3 DRIVES TO THE BASKET. REMEMBER TO SET GOALS THAT ARE ACHIEVABLE BASED ON YOUR SKILL LEVEL. SPEND TIME VISUALIZING YOURSELF PERFORMING AT YOUR BEST AND MENTALLY PREPARING TO EXECUTE THOSE ACTIONS. ENHANCING YOUR PHYSICAL CONDITIONING THROUGH STRENGTH TRAINING, ENDURANCE WORKOUTS, AND AGILITY DRILLS WILL ENABLE YOU TO BRING MORE ENERGY TO YOUR PERFORMANCE. STAY MENTALLY FOCUSED BY USING POSITIVE SELF-TALK TO KEEP CONCENTRATION,

ESPECIALLY IN HIGH-PRESSURE SITUATIONS. EMBRACE COMPETITION BY TREATING EVERY PRACTICE AND GAME AS AN OPPORTUNITY TO GIVE YOUR ALL, AND REMEMBER THAT YOUR INTENSITY IMPACTS YOUR TEAMMATES, MOTIVATING YOU TO PLAY HARD FOR THEM. MANAGE YOUR EMOTIONS BY CHANNELING THEM INTO YOUR PERFORMANCE, WHETHER IT'S EXCITEMENT, DETERMINATION, OR FRUSTRATION. PRACTICE GAME SITUATIONS TO BECOME COMFORTABLE WITH HIGH-PRESSURE SCENARIOS, AND FOCUS ON MASTERING THE FUNDAMENTAL SKILLS OF YOUR SPORT, AS CONFIDENCE IN YOUR SKILLS CREATES MORE INTENSE PLAY. REFLECT ON YOUR PERFORMANCE AFTER GAMES OR PRACTICES TO IDENTIFY AREAS FOR IMPROVEMENT, COMMITTING TO PUSH YOURSELF FURTHER IN THOSE AREAS. BY INTEGRATING THESE STRATEGIES INTO YOUR TRAINING AND COMPETITION, YOU CAN ENHANCE YOUR INTENSITY AND ELEVATE YOUR OVERALL PERFORMANCE.

SUCCESS IS NOT ONLY ABOUT WINNING; IT IS ABOUT HAVING A MINDSET THAT LOVES CHALLENGES, HANDLES TOUGH TIMES, AND ALWAYS LOOKS FOR WAYS TO GET BETTER. STICK TO REGULAR TRAINING, ALONG WITH KEEPING A POSITIVE ATTITUDE, AND INSTILLING A POSITIVE MINDSET;

LET THAT BECOME YOUR THING. REMEMBER, IMPROVEMENT TAKES TIME AND DEDICATION. CELEBRATING PROGRESS AND LEARNING FROM MISTAKES ARE KEY TO BUILDING A STRONG MINDSET. EVENTUALLY, YOU WILL REALIZE THAT HOW YOU THINK IS JUST AS IMPORTANT AS HOW YOU PLAY.

AS WE WRAP UP THIS JOURNEY TOGETHER, REMEMBER THAT HAVING A POSITIVE MINDSET AND WORKING HARD CAN MAKE ALL THE DIFFERENCE IN YOUR SPORTS AND LIFE. EVERY CHALLENGE YOU FACE, WHETHER IT'S A TOUGH GAME, A MISTAKE, OR A SETBACK, IS A CHANCE TO GROW AND BECOME STRONGER. THERE IS ALWAYS A POSITIVE TAKE AWAY FROM A MISTAKE BECAUSE EACH ONE OFFERS A CHANCE TO LEARN, GROW, AND CHANGE. MISTAKES REVEAL GAPS IN UNDERSTANDING OR AREAS THAT NEED IMPROVEMENT, WHICH CAN GUIDE YOU TO MAKE BETTER DECISIONS NEXT TIME. SPORTS ARE NOT JUST ABOUT WINNING; THEY'RE ABOUT LEARNING, BUILDING FRIENDSHIPS, AND MAKING GREAT MEMORIES. SO, WHEN YOU STEP ONTO THE FIELD OR COURT, DO IT WITH CONFIDENCE AND TRUST IN YOUR ABILITIES. DON'T FORGET, EVERY ATHLETE GOES THROUGH UPS AND DOWNS, BUT IT'S HOW YOU RESPOND THAT COUNTS. IF YOU CHOOSE TO REACT IN A POSITIVE WAY, KEEP PUSHING FORWARD, AND WORK TO GET BETTER,

YOU CAN TURN EVERY CHALLENGE INTO A CHANCE TO GROW AND SUCCEED. COACHES WILL SEE THIS AS A SIGN OF MENTAL TOUGHNESS AND DEDICATION. THEY WILL NOTICE A PLAYER WHO DOES NOT GET STUCK ON MISTAKES BUT INSTEAD USES THEM TO IMPROVE. THIS SHOWS COACHES THAT YOU ARE OPEN TO LEARNING, QUICK TO BOUNCE BACK, AND COMMITTED TO GETTING BETTER, QUALITIES THAT WILL MAKE YOU A REAL ASSET TO ANY TEAM.

KEEP PUSHING YOURSELF, SUPPORT YOUR TEAMMATES, AND STAY FOCUSED ON YOUR GOALS. BELIEVE IN YOURSELF BECAUSE YOU HAVE THE POWER TO ACHIEVE AMAZING THINGS. THE JOURNEY DOESN'T END HERE; IT'S JUST THE BEGINNING. EMBRACE EVERY MOMENT, STAY POSITIVE, AND REMEMBER THAT YOUR HARD WORK WILL PAY OFF. YOU'VE GOT THIS!

"HARD TIMES DON'T COME TO BREAK YOU, THEY COME TO HELP YOU GROW."

-DAWN HANCOCK, CEO MĪPOH

JOURNALING

IN THE NEXT PAGES, YOU WILL FIND SPACE TO WRITE ABOUT YOUR OWN SPORTS JOURNEY. USE THESE JOURNAL PAGES TO SHARE YOUR EXPERIENCES, SET GOALS, AND THINK ABOUT WAYS TO IMPROVE YOUR MINDSET. THIS IS YOUR CHANCE TO REFLECT, GROW, AND TAKE STEPS TOWARD BECOMING THE BEST VERSION OF YOURSELF. THIS IS YOUR JOURNEY, MAKE IT YOUR OWN!

"GIVE 100 PERCENT, 100 PERCENT OF THE TIME."

-NOELL GRANT, AUTHOR

MY JOURNAL

MY JOURNAL

MY JOURNAL

MY JOURNAL

MY JOURNAL

MY JOURNAL

MY JOURNAL

MY JOURNAL

MY JOURNAL

MY JOURNAL

NOELL GRANT
BOWIE STATE UNIVERSITY,
1996-1997

HALL OF FAME
BOWIE STATE UNIVERSITY,
1996-1997

CIAA TOURNAMENT CHAMPIONS
BOWIE STATE UNIVERSITY,
1996-1997

AS AN ATHLETE, I PLAYED BASKETBALL, SOFTBALL, RAN TRACK, AND CROSS-COUNTRY. I FINISHED MY 9TH GRADE TRACK SEASON UNDEFEATED, RUNNING A 12-SECOND 100 METERS, A 27-SECOND 200 METERS, AND A 59-SECOND 400 METERS. TO PUT THAT INTO PERSPECTIVE, THAT WAS ONLY 0.87 SECONDS SLOWER THAN THE NATIONAL HIGH SCHOOL RECORD IN THE 100M THAT YEAR. MY TRACK CAREER ENDED AFTER 9TH GRADE DUE TO HEADACHES AND NAUSEA AFTER MOST MEETS. YEARS LATER, I REALIZED THAT I WAS LIKELY OVEREXERTING MYSELF AND NOT STAYING HYDRATED, WHICH CAUSED MY POST-MEET DISCOMFORT.

AS A VARSITY BASKETBALL PLAYER AT GAITHERSBURG HIGH SCHOOL, I LED MY TEAM IN STEALS AND POINTS, AVERAGING 14 POINTS AND 4.6 STEALS PER GAME. MY SEASON HIGH WAS 25 POINTS. I WAS NAMED ALL-COUNTY, MVP TWO YEARS IN A ROW, MY TEAM WON OUR DIVISION CHAMPIONSHIP, AND I TOOK MY TEAM TO THE STATE TOURNAMENT. DESPITE A STANDOUT HIGH SCHOOL BASKETBALL CAREER, I HAD TO ATTEND JUNIOR COLLEGE (JUCO) DUE TO MY POOR GRADES, WHICH SERVES AS A REMINDER THAT WE ARE STUDENTS FIRST AND ATHLETES SECOND. YOU CAN BE THE MOST TALENTED PLAYER OR A TOP 10 DIVISION I RECRUIT, BUT WITHOUT THE NECESSARY GRADES, YOU WILL NOT GET INTO THE COLLEGE OF YOUR CHOICE.

NOELL GRANT
NATIONAL JUCO TOURNAMENT
RUNNER-UPS

THE 1992-1993 SEASON, THE YEAR BEFORE I ARRIVED AT MONTGOMERY COLLEGE-ROCKVILLE, THE WOMEN'S BASKETBALL TEAM WENT 0-6 BEFORE BECOMING DEFUNCT. DURING MY FRESHMAN SEASON IN 1993-1994, I AVERAGED 16 POINTS, 8 REBOUNDS, AND 5.2 STEALS PER GAME. MY HIGH REBOUND AVERAGE WASN'T BECAUSE I WAS TALL, STANDING AT ONLY 5'7"3/4 IT WAS BECAUSE I HAD HEART, GRIT, AND DETERMINATION, SOMETHING I HOPE TO INSPIRE IN YOU BY READING MY BOOK. I REMEMBER ONE GAME WHERE I HAD 19 REBOUNDS. THE CROWD WAS GOING CRAZY, SCREAMING FOR ME TO GET 20. I NEVER GOT THERE, BUT IT GOES TO SHOW YOU, IT'S NOT ALL ABOUT SCORING HIGH POINTS. JUST MASTER WHAT YOU ARE GOOD AT. I WAS THE TEAM'S MVP, THE SCHOOL'S FEMALE ATHLETE OF THE YEAR, I LED MY TEAM TO ITS FIRST EVER NATIONAL TOURNAMENT, AND WE FINISHED THE SEASON 8TH IN THE NATION. I WAS NAMED TO THE MARYLAND JUCO ALL-CONFERENCE TEAM AND NATIONAL JUNIOR COLLEGE ATHLETIC ASSOCIATION ALL-AMERICAN TEAM.

IN MARCH 1994, I REMEMBER TRAVELING TO THE JUCO NATIONAL TOURNAMENT IN CORNING,

ABOUT THE AUTHOR

NEW YORK. WE WERE DRIVING THROUGH A SNOWSTORM WITH LITTLE VISIBILITY. I HEARD MY COACH SAY, "HERE WE GO!" AS OUR TEAM VAN SLID OFF THE ROADWAY AND FLIPPED OVER TWICE. AS THE VAN CAME TO A STOP, ONE OF MY TEAMMATES WAS HANGING HALFWAY OUT OF A BROKEN WINDOW WITH A HUGE GASH IN HER THIGH THAT REQUIRED SEVERAL STITCHES. HALF OF OUR TEAM WAS SEEN AT A LOCAL HOSPITAL AND RELEASED THAT EVENING. WE WERE ALL IN SHOCK, BANGED UP, SCARED AND STRANDED. HOWEVER, WE HAD EACH OTHER, AND WE WERE ALL DETERMINED TO FINISH THE REMARKABLE SEASON WE WERE HAVING. DESPITE THE INCIDENT, WE CONTINUED TO THE TOURNAMENT WITH ONLY SEVEN PLAYERS AND MADE IT TO THE CHAMPIONSHIP GAME. DUE TO THE INJURIES FROM THE ACCIDENT AND FOUL TROUBLE, WE FINISHED THE GAME WITH 2 PLAYERS ON THE COURT. ALTHOUGH WE LOST, THE DETERMINATION AND PERSEVERANCE WE SHOWED TO PLAY IN OUR SCHOOL'S FIRST-EVER NATIONAL TOURNAMENT WAS NOTHING SHORT OF REMARKABLE. WE ALL HAVE DETERMINATION AND WILL WITHIN US. SOMETIMES IT TAKES A TRAGIC EVENT OR THE WILL TO SURVIVE TO BRING IT OUT. WITH THE RIGHT MINDSET, YOU CAN HARNESS IT AT ANY TIME.

AFTER JUCO, I EARNED A SCHOLARSHIP TO ATTEND BOWIE STATE UNIVERSITY. BOWIE STATE HAD A BASKETBALL RECORD OF JUST 1-22 THREE YEARS PRIOR. THE YEAR I GOT THERE, WE FINISHED WITH A RECORD OF 22-8. THE FOLLOWING YEAR, WE FINISHED THE SEASON WITH AN ASTOUNDING RECORD OF 30-2, ALONG WITH THE SCHOOL'S FIRST CONFERENCE CHAMPIONSHIP. OUR TEAM WAS A FORCE TO BE RECKONED WITH. TRAINING BY RUNNING ON THE TRACK, HILLS, AND BLEACHERS; DOING CALISTHENICS; LIFTING WEIGHTS; UNDERGOING STEM THERAPY; AND PARTICIPATING IN CROSS-COUNTRY MEETS PREPARED US TO WIN TITLES, BREAK RECORDS, WIN CHAMPIONSHIPS, AND GAIN NATIONAL NOTORIETY. WE WERE NAMED #2 IN THE NATION IN SCORING DEFENSE, A STAT WE WERE VERY PROUD OF. THAT YEAR, WE MADE IT TO THE NCAA SWEET 16, AND WERE THE MOST WINNING TEAM IN SCHOOL HISTORY. WE STARTED A STRONG LEGACY OF WINNING, CREATED BY THE MINDSET THAT THIS WAS A CHAMPIONSHIP PROGRAM. IN THE FOLLOWING YEARS, TWO MORE CHAMPIONSHIPS WERE WON WITH IMPRESSIVE RECORDS OF 29-2 AND 25-4, RESPECTIVELY.

THE FIRE WE STARTED KEPT BURNING AND RESULTED IN A THREE-PEAT OF OUR CONFERENCE CHAMPIONSHIP!

ABOUT THE AUTHOR

THESE ACHIEVEMENTS EARNED MY TEAM A PLACE IN THE BOWIE STATE SPORTS HALL OF FAME. IT WAS DURING THESE YEARS THAT I LEARNED TO COMPETE AT A HIGH LEVEL AND DEVELOPED A MINDSET WHERE LOSING WAS NOT AN OPTION. OUR PRACTICES WERE INTENSE, DESIGNED TO PUSH OURSELVES AND OUR TEAMMATES TO BE BETTER, MAKING THE GAMES FEEL EASY BY COMPARISON. THIS MINDSET IS WHAT I AIM TO INSTILL IN YOU THROUGHOUT THIS BOOK. INTERESTINGLY, I NEVER INTENDED TO RUN CROSS-COUNTRY; IT WAS A REQUIREMENT FROM MY STRICT COLLEGE COACHES, DESPITE MY DISLIKE FOR LONG DISTANCE RUNNING. IN HIGH SCHOOL, I EVEN TOLD A TEAMMATE I WOULD NEVER RUN CROSS-COUNTRY, YET FOUR YEARS LATER, SHE FOUND MY NAME IN THE PAPER FOR AN OUTSTANDING COLLEGIATE CROSS-COUNTRY MEET PERFORMANCE. MIKE TYSON'S QUOTE, "DISCIPLINE IS DOING WHAT YOU HATE TO DO BUT DOING IT LIKE YOU LOVE IT," WAS EXACTLY MY MINDSET AT THE TIME. I BELIEVE EVERYONE CAN FIND THEIR SOURCE OF MOTIVATION, AND WITH IT, THE POWER OF A POSITIVE MINDSET.

AFTER GRADUATING WITH A BACHELOR'S DEGREE IN SOCIOLOGY, I TRANSITIONED TO COACHING HIGH SCHOOL AND AAU BASKETBALL. I NOW TRAIN MY DAUGHTER, WHO COMPETES IN HIGH SCHOOL

AND AAU BASKETBALL. AS THE FORMER COO OF MIPOH, I HELPED ORGANIZATIONS IMPROVE PERFORMANCE, CULTURE AND RETENTION BY EMPOWERING EMPLOYEES TO LIVE HAPPIER LIVES THROUGH WELLNESS PIT-STOPS, WORKSHOPS, AND POP-UPS. ADDITIONALLY, I AM THE FOUNDER/DIRECTOR OF BEYOND YOUR BLOCK, A NONPROFIT ORGANIZATION DEDICATED TO TAKING YOUTH BEYOND THE BOUNDARIES OF THEIR NEIGHBORHOODS. WE EXPOSE YOUTH TO DIVERSE EXPERIENCES AND CULTURES, HELPING THEM DEVELOP INTO STRONG-MINDED, INDEPENDENT, AND POSITIVE MEMBERS OF SOCIETY. I HOPE YOU ENJOY MY BOOK AND TAKE AWAY VALUABLE LESSONS THAT HELP YOU GROW, BOTH ON AND OFF THE COURT. MY GOAL IS TO INSPIRE YOU TO SHIFT YOUR MINDSET, EMBRACE CHALLENGES, AND REACH YOUR FULL POTENTIAL. THANK YOU FOR READING!

NOELL GRANT

My Athletic

Journey

TO MY DAUGHTERS, ASHLEY, ALEXIS, AND PAYTON: I HOPE THIS BOOK INSPIRES YOU AND OPENS YOUR MINDS ON YOUR JOURNEY TO SUCCESS. YOU BOTH ARE MY INSPIRATION FOR WRITING THIS BOOK, AND I AM SO PROUD OF YOU.

TO MY HUSBAND, RED: THANK YOU FOR YOUR LOVE, SUPPORT, AND GUIDANCE. YOU ALWAYS PUSH ME TO GROW AND NEVER STAY COMFORTABLE. YOU ARE MY REASSURANCE THAT I CAN ACHIEVE ANYTHING I PUT MY MIND TO.

TO MY PARENTS, YOU INSTILLED A POWERFUL MINDSET IN ME AT AN EARLY AGE, MAKING MY SPORTS JOURNEY POSSIBLE. YOU BELIEVED IN ME AND SUPPORTED ME EVERY STEP OF THE WAY, ALWAYS CHEERING ME ON AT COMPETITIONS. MOM, I KNOW YOU'RE WATCHING OVER ME AND CHEERING FROM HEAVEN. (RIP, MAY 15, 2022)

TO MY FRIEND, DAWN: THIS BOOK WOULD NOT EXIST WITHOUT YOU. CREATING MĪPOH (MY PURSUIT OF HAPPINESS) GAVE ME THE MINDSET TO WRITE THIS BOOK. YOUR WORDS, WISDOM, AND GUIDANCE ARE POWERFUL, AND THEY HELPED ME IMMENSELY WITH MY WRITINGS. THE WORLD NEEDS TO EXPERIENCE YOU.

I WOULD LIKE TO EXTEND MY DEEPEST GRATITUDE TO DR. TAMMY WILLIAMS FOR HER EXCEPTIONAL EDITORIAL SUPPORT ON THIS BOOK. TAMMY, YOUR EXPERTISE AND SUPPORT HAVE TRULY ELEVATED THIS PROJECT, AND FOR THAT, I AM INCREDIBLY GRATEFUL.

REFERENCES   *139*

Page 1. Allen Iverson press conference: May 7, 2022
https://youtu.be/K9ZQhyOZCNE?si=JzLq7rFNwjnLIERw

Page 15. Sanders, D. The Life Pedia. (n.d.). Posted by The Life Pedia on
Instagram: [https://www.instagram.com/reel/C69aRJRS7D_/?
igsh=eHZrc2Qya3ZqbmZx]
(https://www.instagram.com/reel/C69aRJRS7D_/?
igsh=eHZrc2Qya3ZqbmZx).

Page 15. Increased Social Comparison:
Vogel, E. A., Rose, J. P., Roberts, L. R., & Eckles, K. (2014). Social
comparison, social media, and self-esteem. Psychology of Popular Media
Culture, 3(4), 206–222. [Link](https://doi.org/10.1037/ppm0000047).

Page 27. Bryant, K. (2021, August 9). Kobe Bryant Shares Unreal Stories
about Michael Jordan. Posted by Piotrekz Production on YouTube:
https://youtu.be/rx0cTkSItpQ.

Page 42. Joey Hewitt, @Findjoeflow
https://www.instagram.com/reel/C_QlCZTv2mZ/?
utm_source=ig_web_button_share_sheet

Page 49. Mickelson, P. (2023, December 1). 33 Quotes on Success (Golf).
Retrieved from Gracious Quotes: [https://graciousquotes.com/phil-
mickelson/](https://graciousquotes.com/phil-mickelson/).

Page 106. Photo by Don Rocky:
https://www.instagram.com/don_rockyy/?
igsh=MThpcGVvMjdjZXdleA%3D%3D

Certain images in this book are used under license for Envato Elements
and are the property of their respective copyright holders.